Colouring Book
Tour
of
St. Kitts
and
Nevis

By Joan Mallalieu

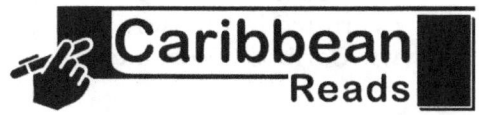

Mrs. Joan Mallalieu is one of St. Kitts' best known artists. She holds a B.A. Fine Arts. She has been recognised as a Patron of the Arts in St. Kitts and has been awarded the National Award for the Development of Arts and Crafts.

Cover and interior illustrations © 2014 by Joan Mallalieu
CaribbeanReads Publishing, Basseterre, St. Kitts
Second Edition
ISBN 978-0990865957
All rights reserved.
Printed in the USA
www.CaribbeanReads.com

About St. Kitts and Nevis

On his second voyage to the Caribbean in 1493, Christopher Columbus sailed past an island which he named St. Christopher because it resembled the shape of St. Christopher carrying the Christ child on his shoulder. The name is usually shortened to St Kitts. Columbus later spotted the island of Nevis which was originally named Nuestra Senora de las Nieves (Lady of the Snows) because of the halo of clouds ever present at the summit of the island's main mountain range. This name was eventually shortened to Nevis.

While Columbus' arrival marked the start of the islands' recorded history, the islands were originally inhabited by Amerindians. Columbus' arrival was followed by the French and the English. Later, people were enslaved and brought from Africa to work on sugar plantations.

Sugar was very important as a cash crop on the islands for centuries until the 1970s when competition from other countries and from sugar substitutes caused the demand for sugar to decline. Sugar is no longer the major industry, having been replaced by tourism, vegetable production, and fishing.

St. Kitts and Nevis achieved independence from Britain in 1983. The first Premier was the Hon. Sir Robert Bradshaw and the first Prime Minister after the Federation achieved independence was the Rt. Hon. Dr. Kennedy Simmonds. At the time of this second edition publication the Prime Minister is the Honourable Dr. Timothy Harris.

The islands are located in the North Eastern part of the Caribbean 17*20 North and 62*45 West. The weather is tropical all the year round with a cooling breeze, summer or winter. The average temperature is 78*F or 25*C with very low humidity.

Some Notes on St Kitts

St. Kitts has an area of 68 square miles with a central mountain range rising from the sea dominated by Mount "Liamuiga", the indigenous peoples' name for the island.

St. Kitts has a modern international airport named for Sir Robert Llewelyn Bradshaw, which is enhanced by facilities for private jets. Large cruise ships regularly dock at Port Zante which was once 20 acres of sea water. Visitors can stay in one of the first-class hotels located on the island.

Places of interest include the Brimstone Hill Fortress National Park—a World Heritage Site dubbed the "Gibraltar of the West Indies", Black Rocks, and the many historic spots in the capital city, Basseterre. Visitors can enjoy a walk through the town, explore the beaches, golf, ride the sugar train, zip line through the rain forests, sail on a catamaran, and much more. Our rich history, along with our culture and climate, makes a visit to this Caribbean island something you will always remember.

There are several American off-shore Medical Universities on the island and one veterinary school.

Sir Thomas Warner who was the British founder of St. Kitts is buried on the grounds of St. Thomas a church in the village of Middle Island.

Some Notes on Nevis

Nevis is known for its white-sand beaches, fishing boats, and restaurants on the beach famous for local drinks and mouth-watering dishes.

Hiking through Nevis is a national pastime whether exploring the lush rain forest or observing the Vervet monkeys that live among the ruins of plantation houses and churches.

Nevis now has the Vance Amory Airport named after its first Premier and deep water facilities for cargo and cruise ships. There are also a number of off -shore Medical Universities which accommodate students from all over the world.

There are now many first class hotels in Nevis. Several of the hotels are developed from old plantation ruins and sugar mills while there are other modern new resorts located on pristine beaches.

Fort Charles was built by the English to protect the city of Charlestown when it was important for its sugar production.

Nevis boasts of the fame of two men who played a part in international history:

Lord Horatio Nelson, Britain's famous Admiral who used Nevis as his base of operations in the mid 1780's and married a Nevisian, Frances Nisbet, in 1787.

Alexander Hamilton, who was born on Nevis on January 11th 1757, became one of the founding fathers of America and Secretary of the Treasury.

St. Kitts-Nevis National Flag

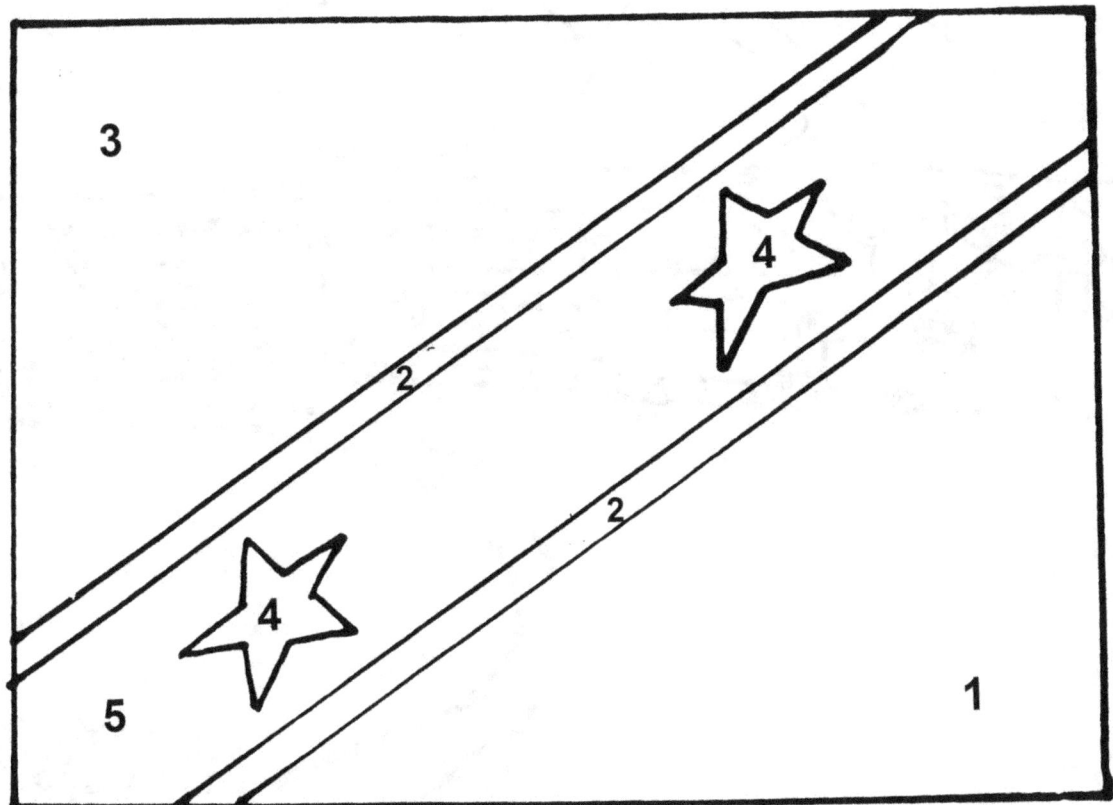

Each colour on the flag has a special meaning.
Follow the numbers and colour the flag.

1-Red-Our fight for freedom
2-Yellow-Year round sunshine
3-Green-The fertile land
4-White-Symbols of hope and liberty
5-Black-Our African heritage

The Sugar Train

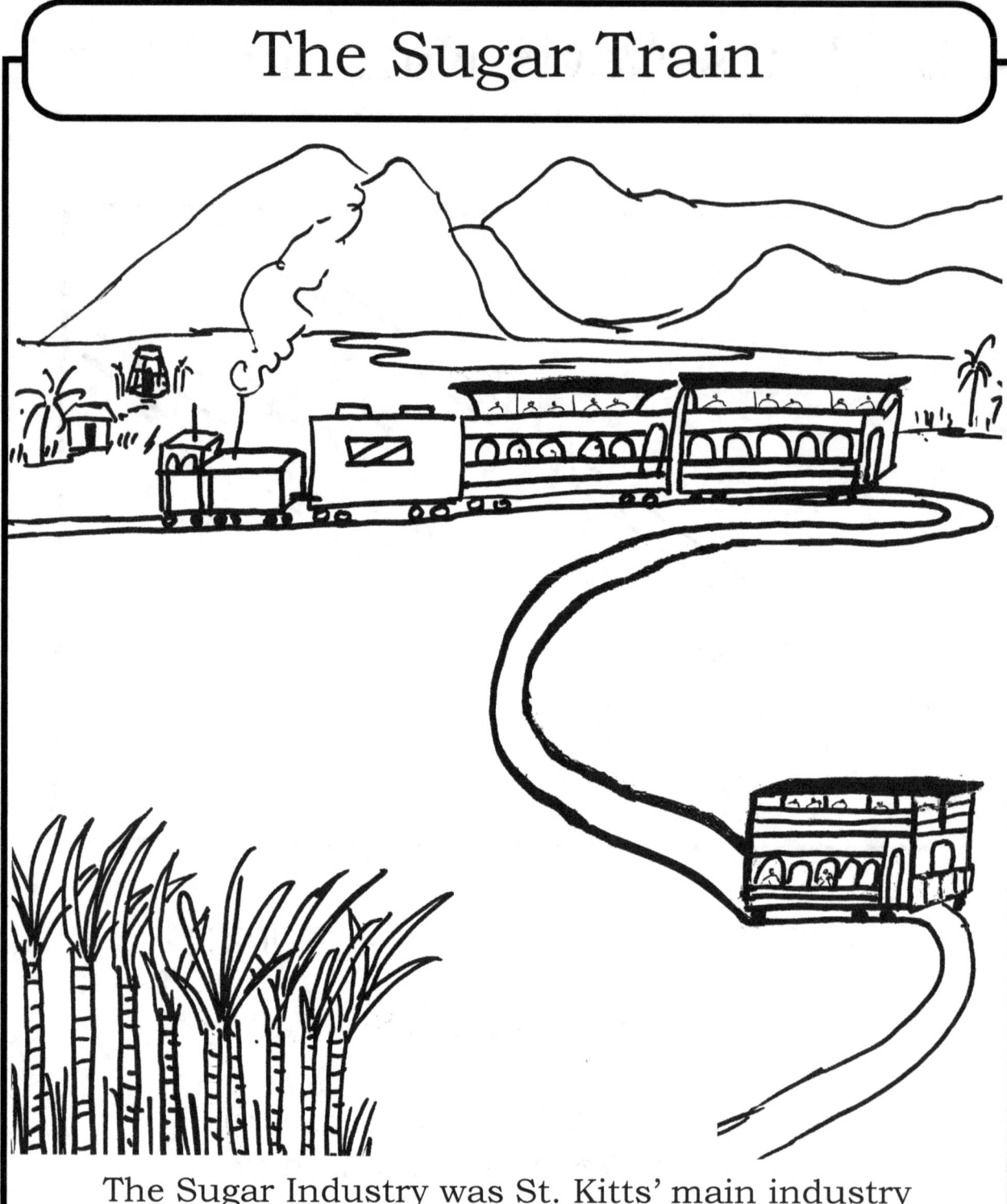

The Sugar Industry was St. Kitts' main industry
until its closure in July 2005. Trains were used
to transport the cut sugar cane from the fields to
the sugar factory and you can ride on a replica of
those trains today.
Be sure to find the St. Kitts Flag!

Sugar Mill

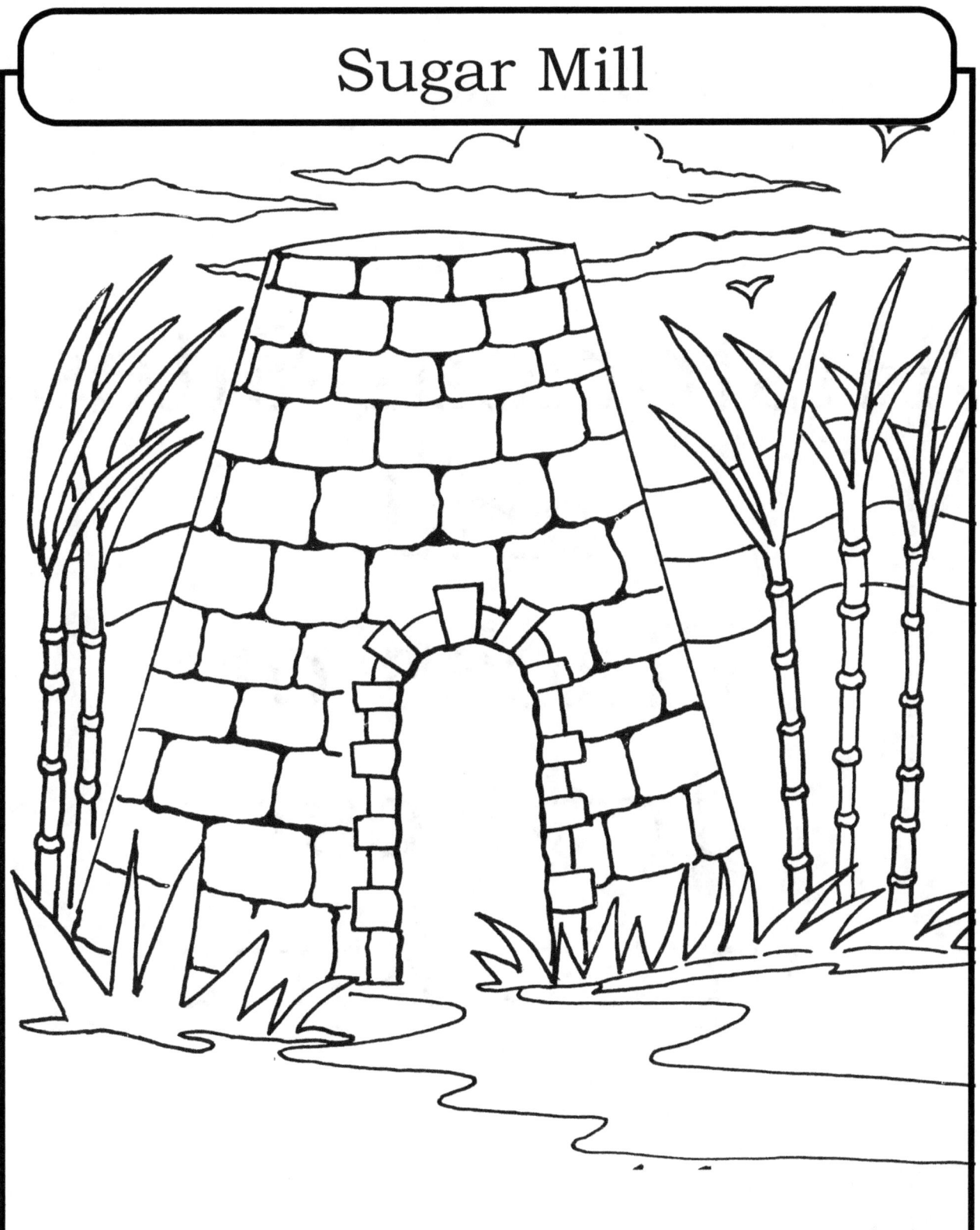

From the 18th to the 20th centuries, sugar mills in St. Kitts and Nevis were used to make sugar from sugar cane.

Historical Sites and Places of Interest in St. Kitts

Brimstone Hill National Fortress Park

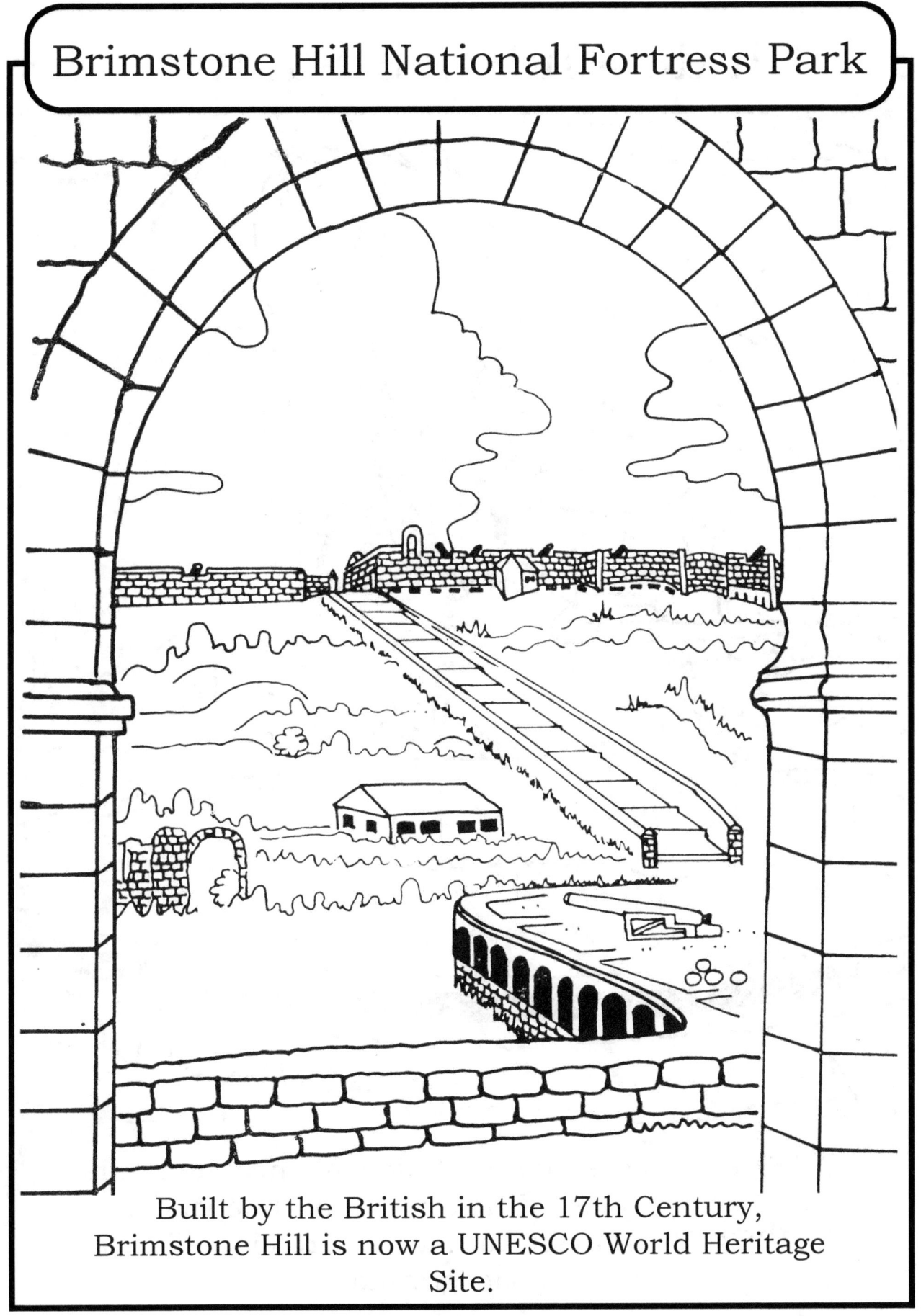

Built by the British in the 17th Century, Brimstone Hill is now a UNESCO World Heritage Site.

Independence Square

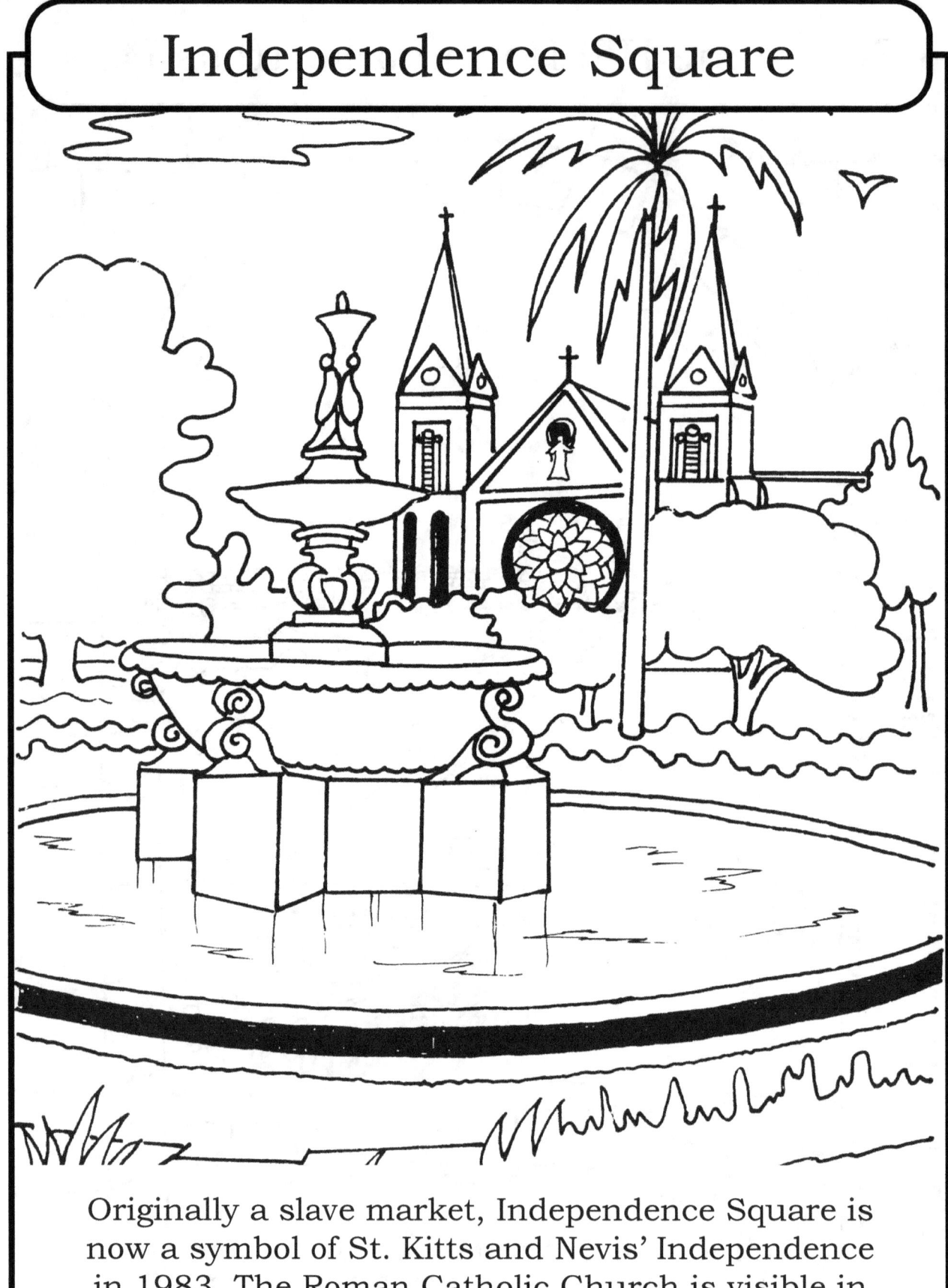

Originally a slave market, Independence Square is now a symbol of St. Kitts and Nevis' Independence in 1983. The Roman Catholic Church is visible in the background.

St. George's Anglican Church

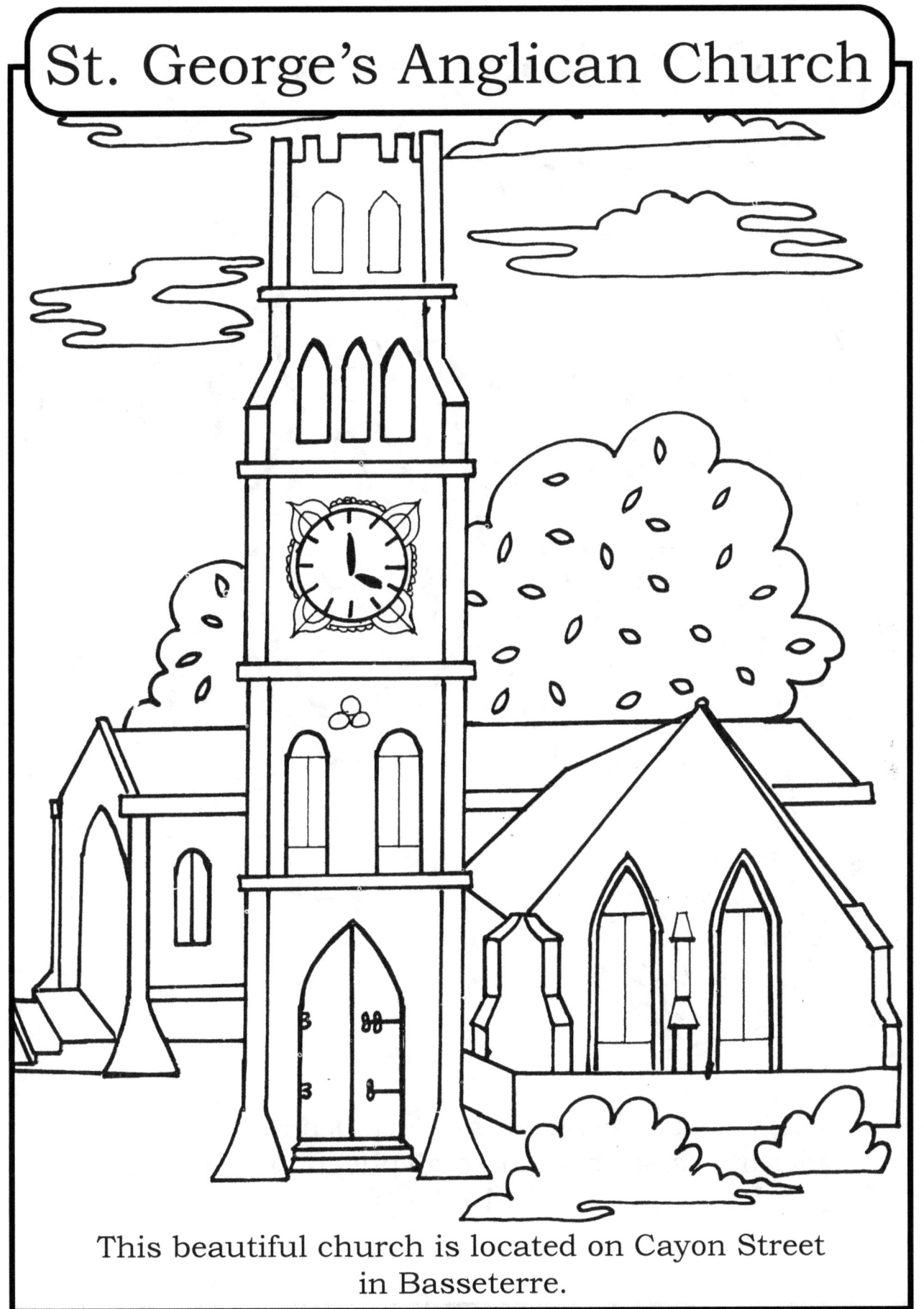

This beautiful church is located on Cayon Street
in Basseterre.

7

Carib Rock Drawings

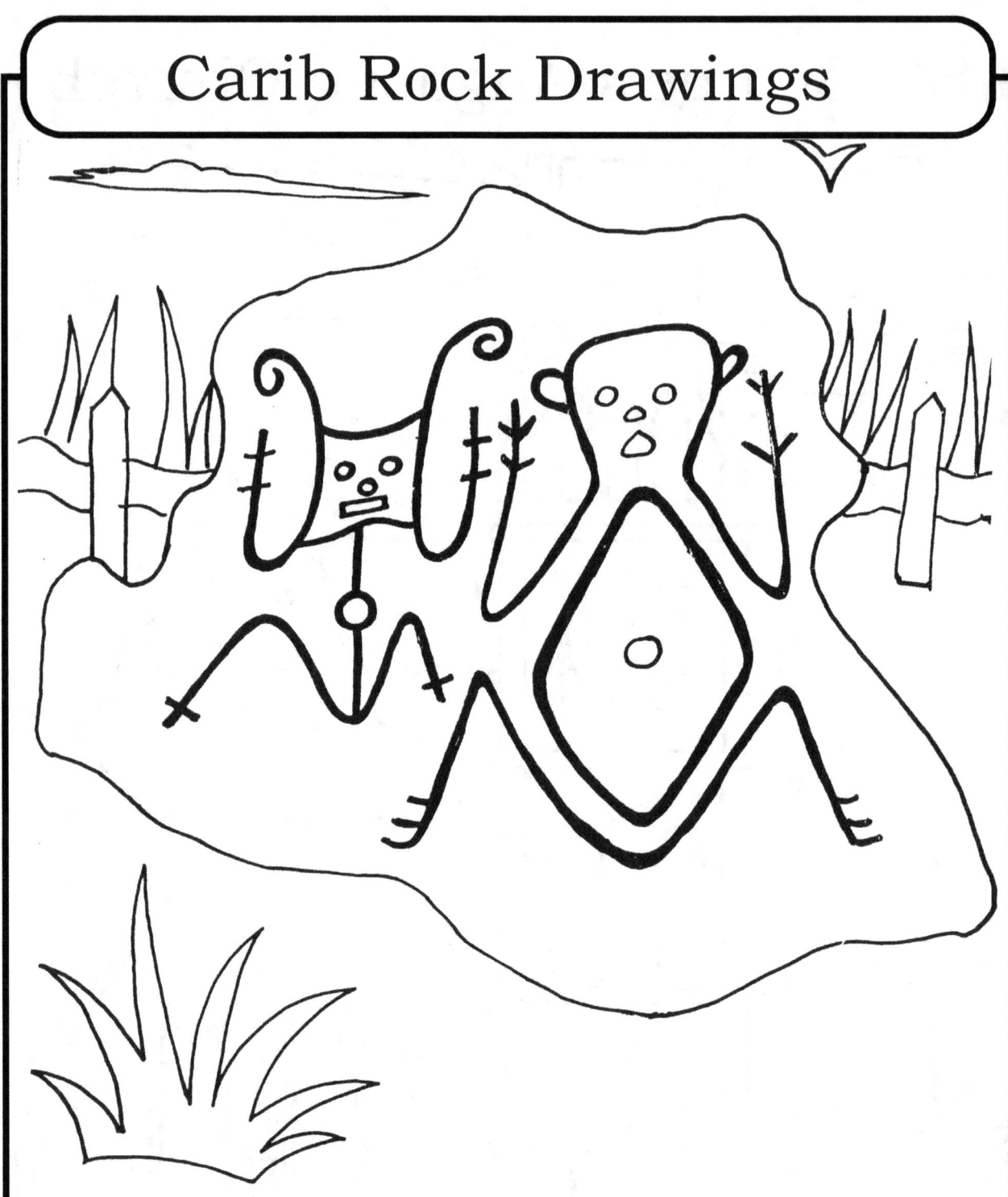

Indigenous people of the Caribbean drew these pictures (also called petroglyphs) on rocks in Old Road Village.

The Cenotaph

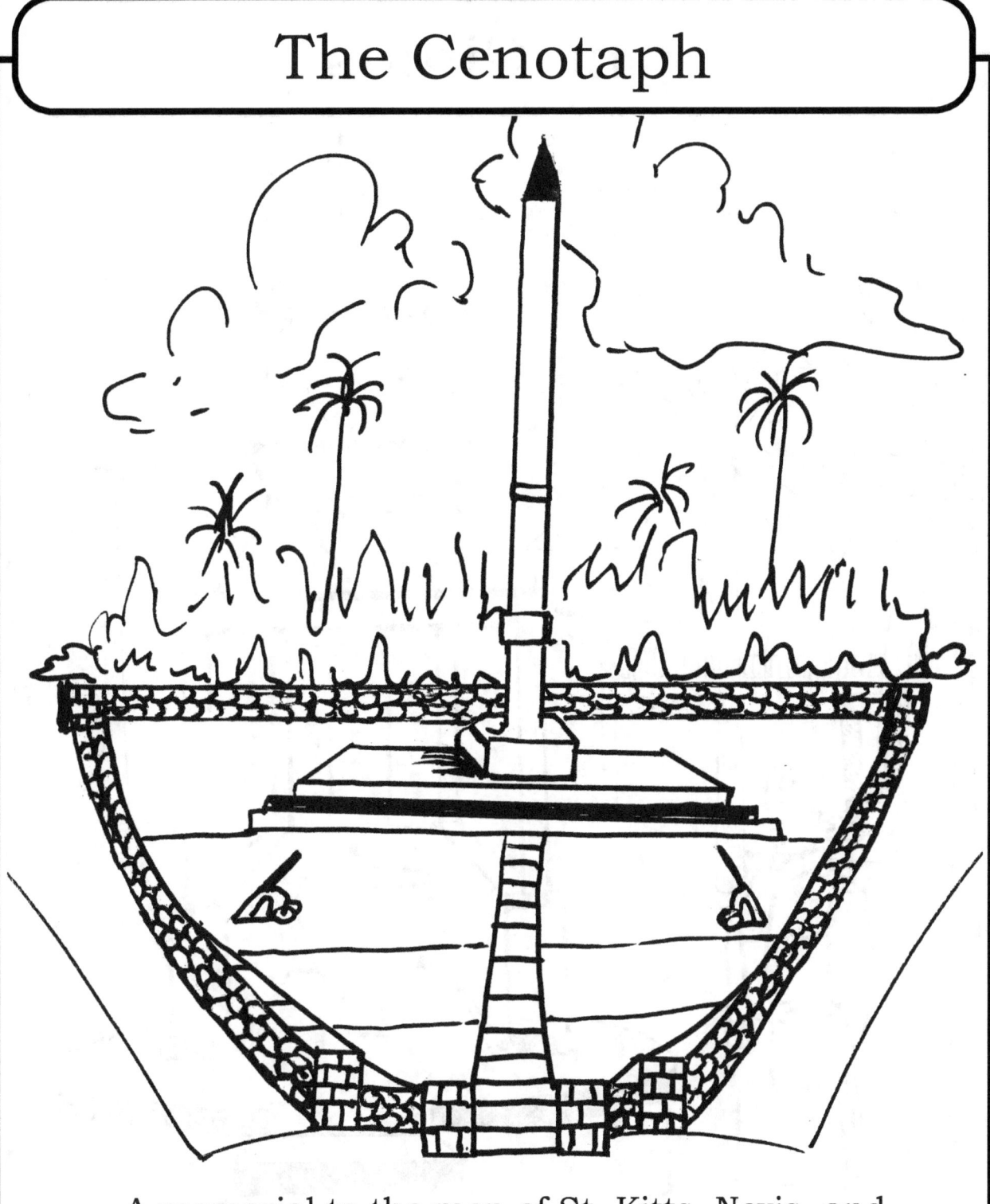

A memorial to the men of St. Kitts, Nevis, and Anguilla who lost their lives in World Wars I and II. Visit it next Veteran's Day, you might find your ancestors among the names engraved on the plaques.

The Circus

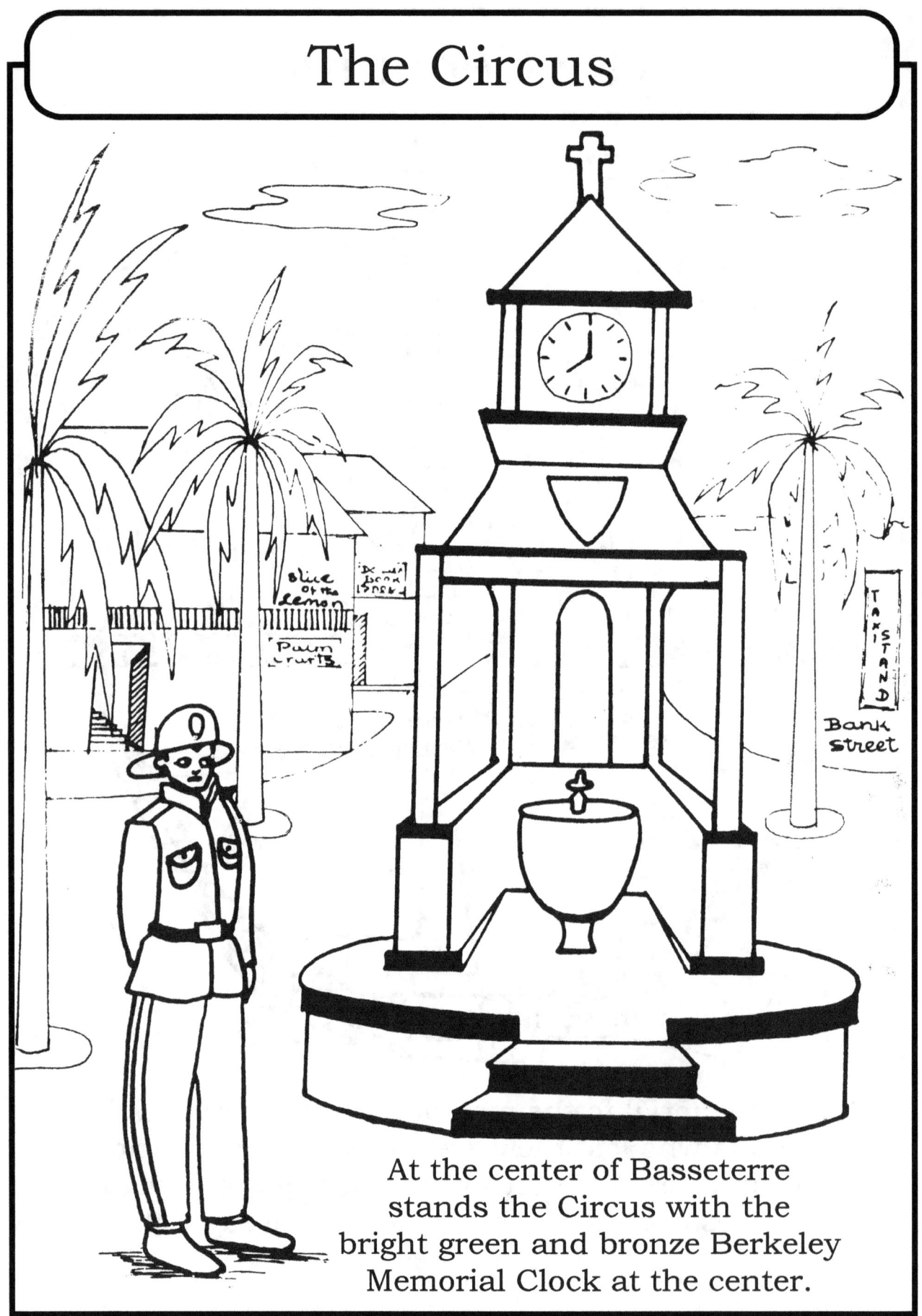

At the center of Basseterre stands the Circus with the bright green and bronze Berkeley Memorial Clock at the center.

The National Museum

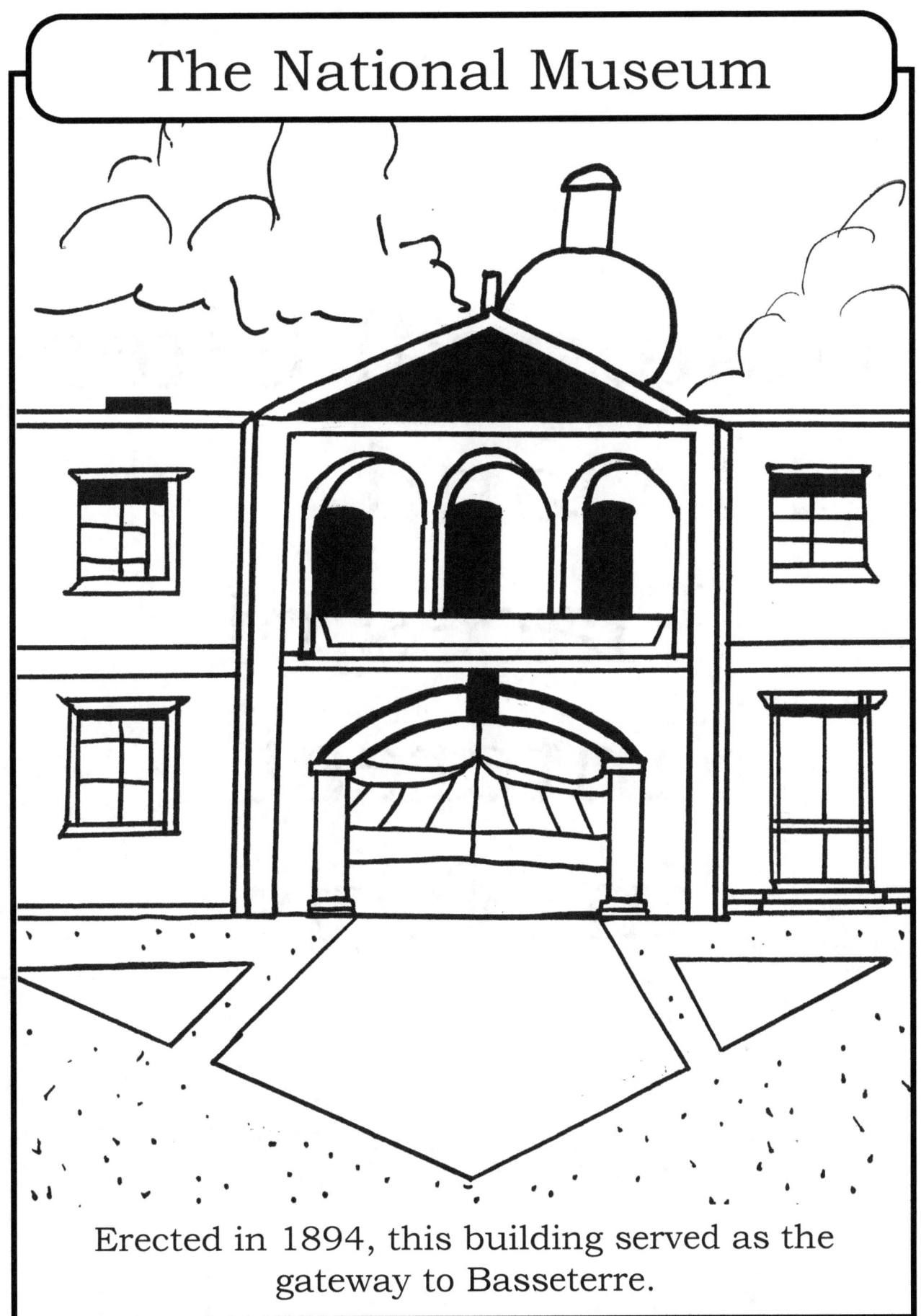

Erected in 1894, this building served as the gateway to Basseterre.

Historical Sites and Places of Interest in Nevis

Memorial Square

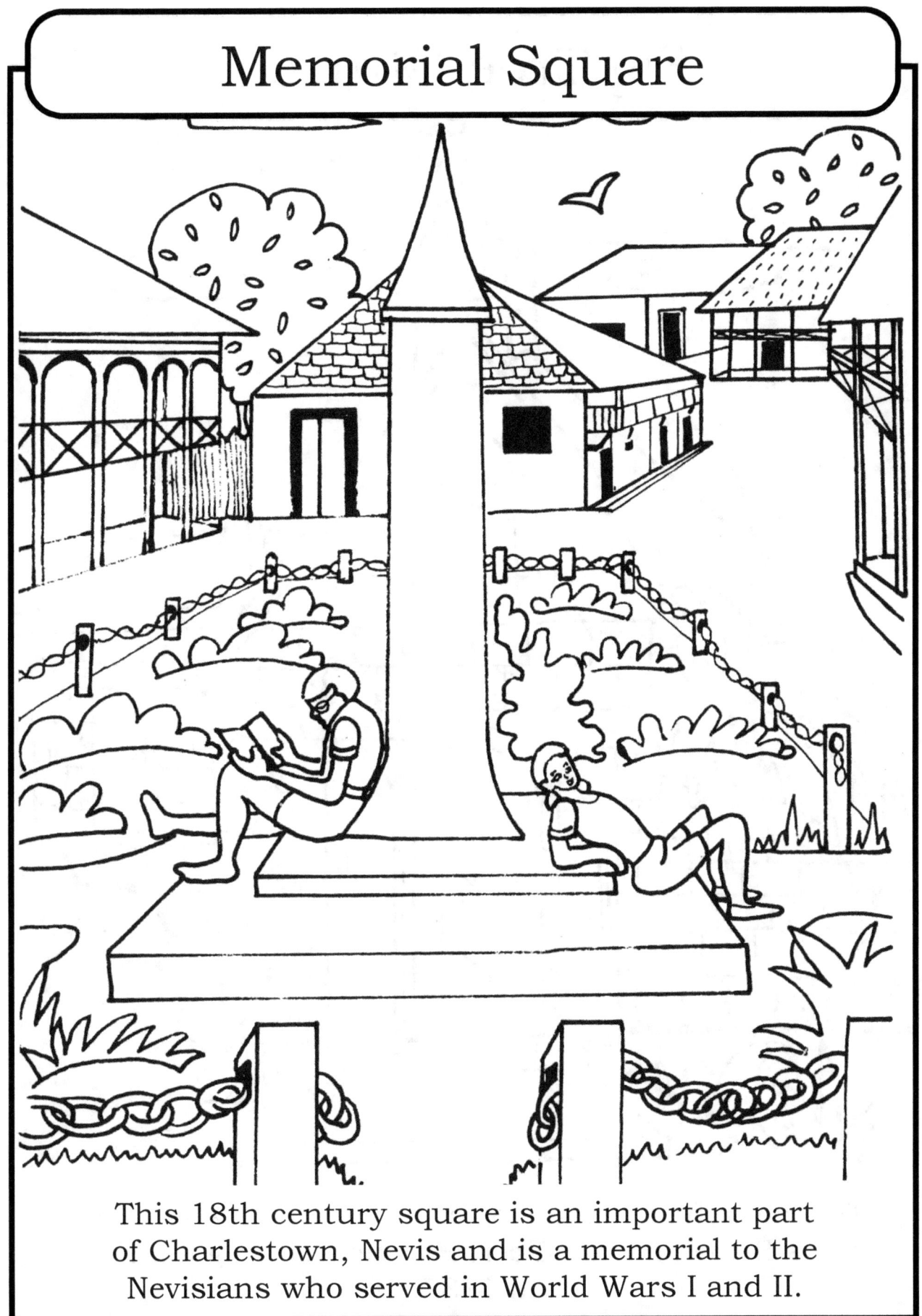

This 18th century square is an important part
of Charlestown, Nevis and is a memorial to the
Nevisians who served in World Wars I and II.

Fig Tree Church

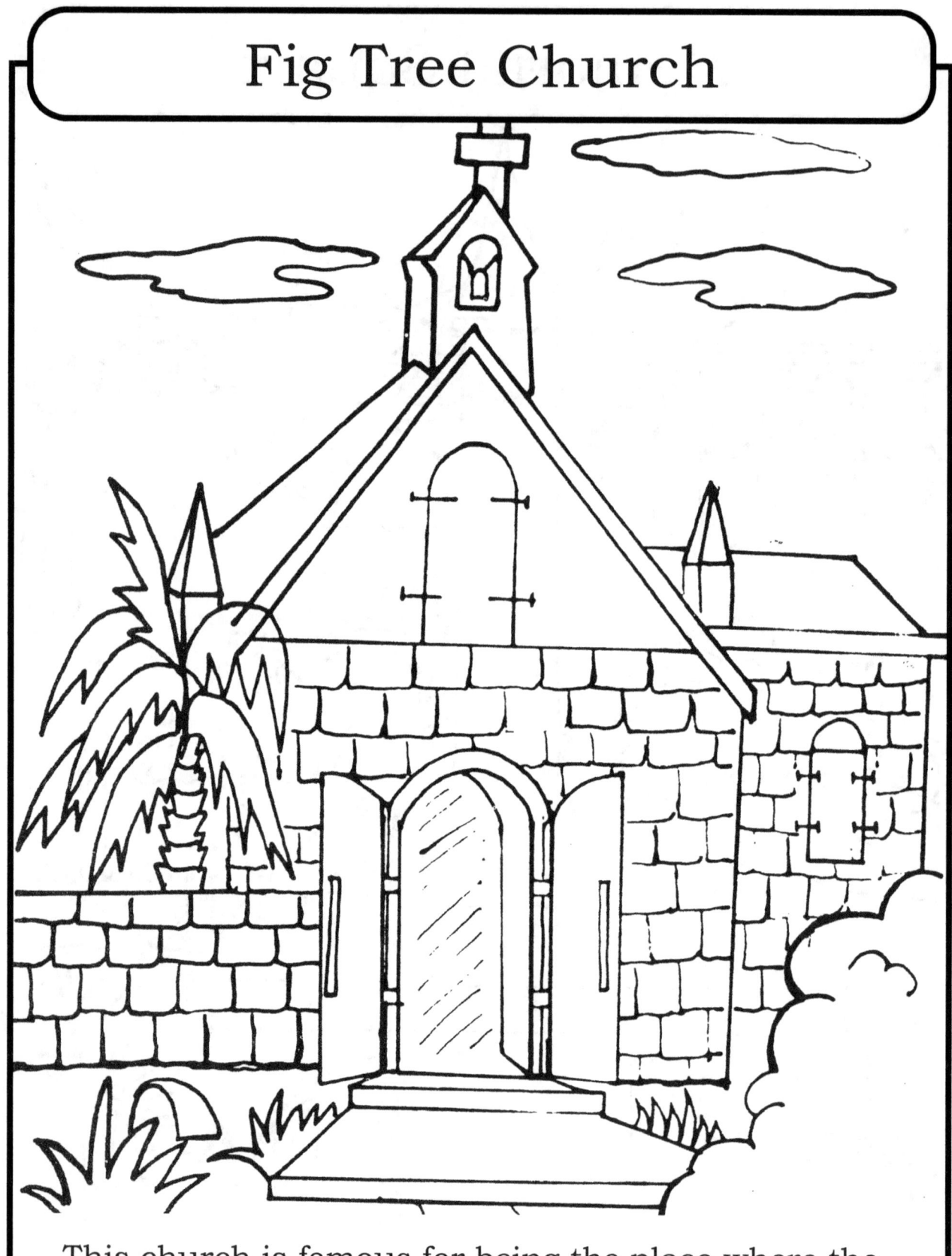

This church is famous for being the place where the famous British naval officer, Horatio Nelson got married in 1787.

Alexander Hamilton's House

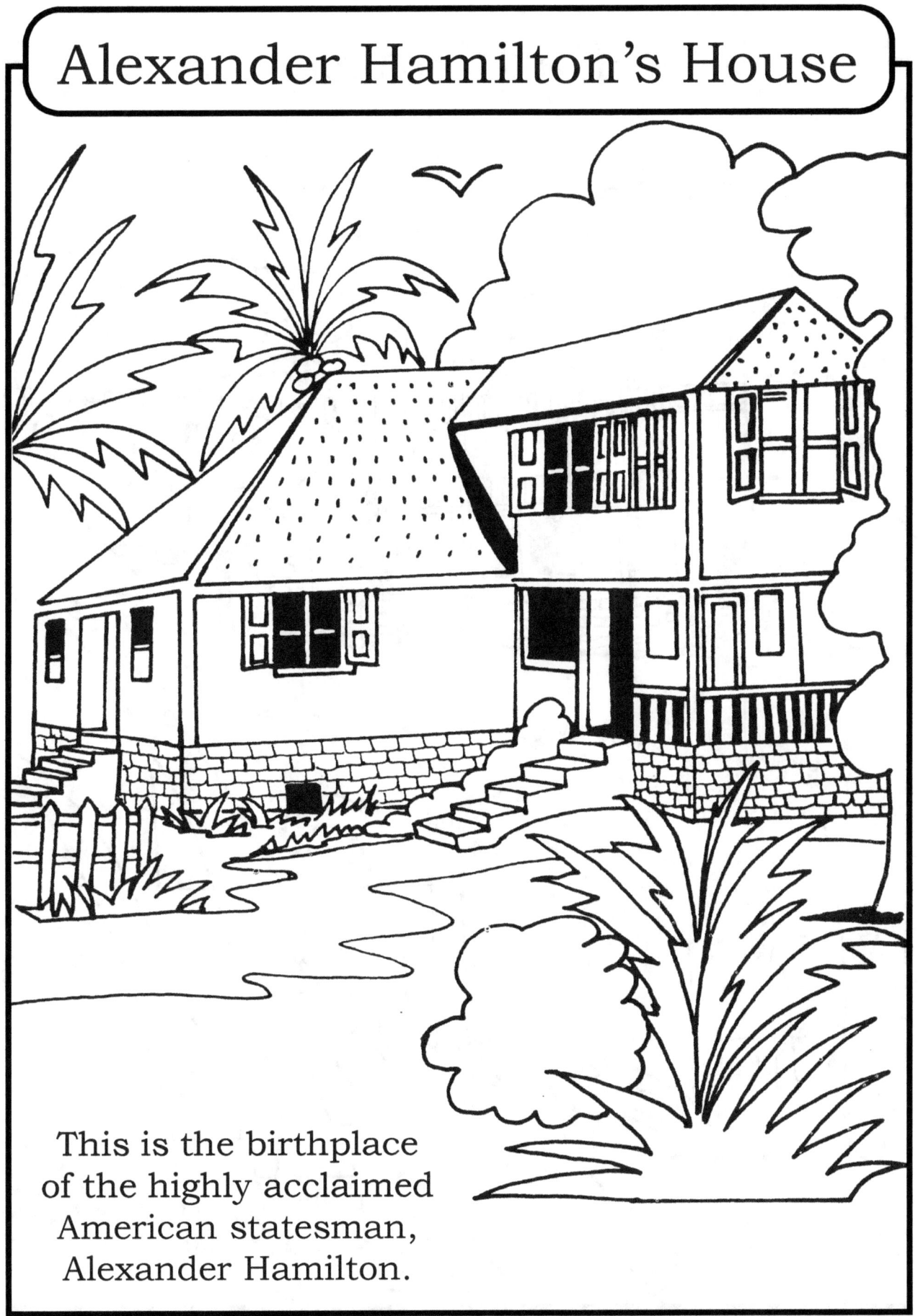

This is the birthplace
of the highly acclaimed
American statesman,
Alexander Hamilton.

Bath Hotel

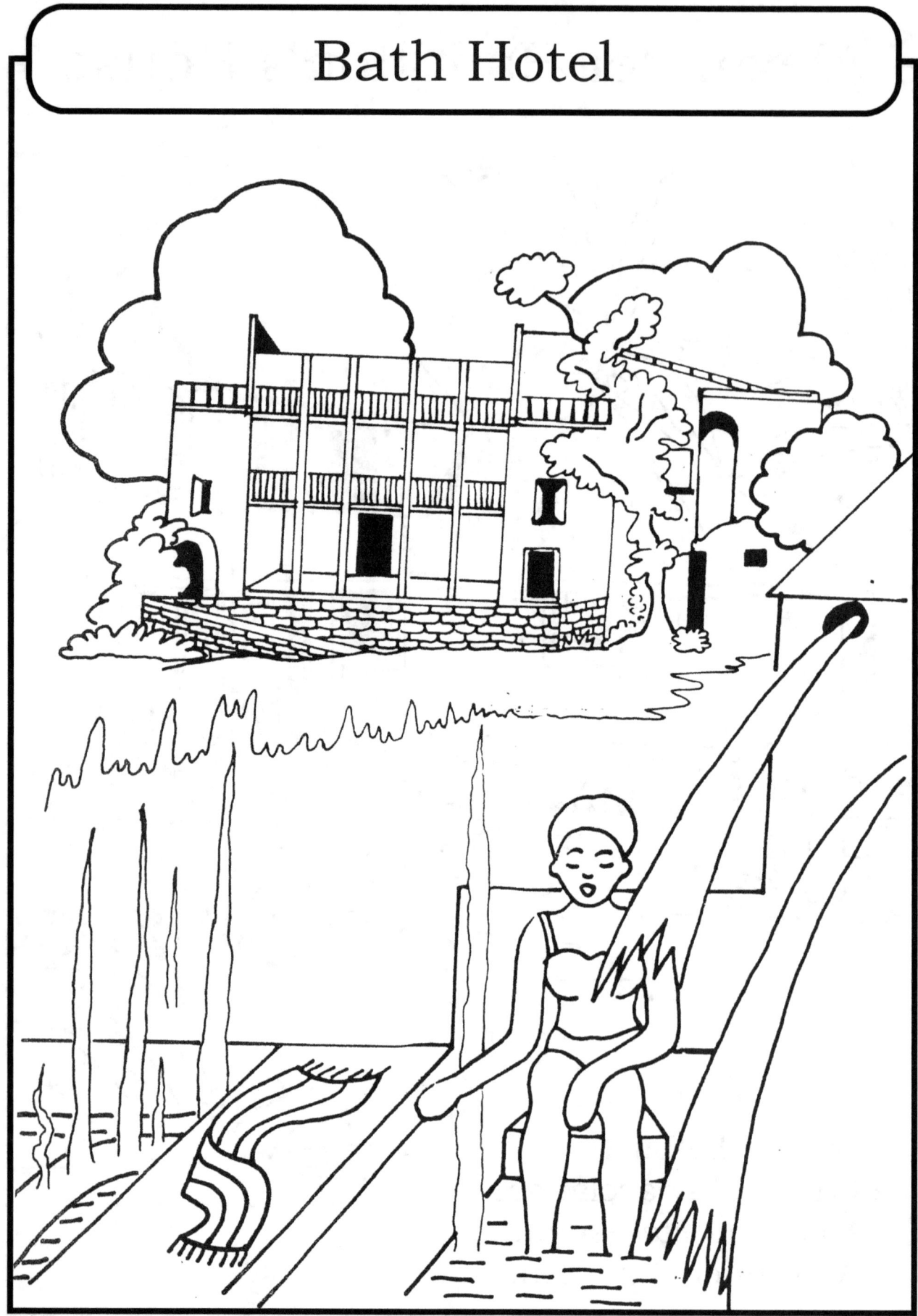

A Nevis Hotel

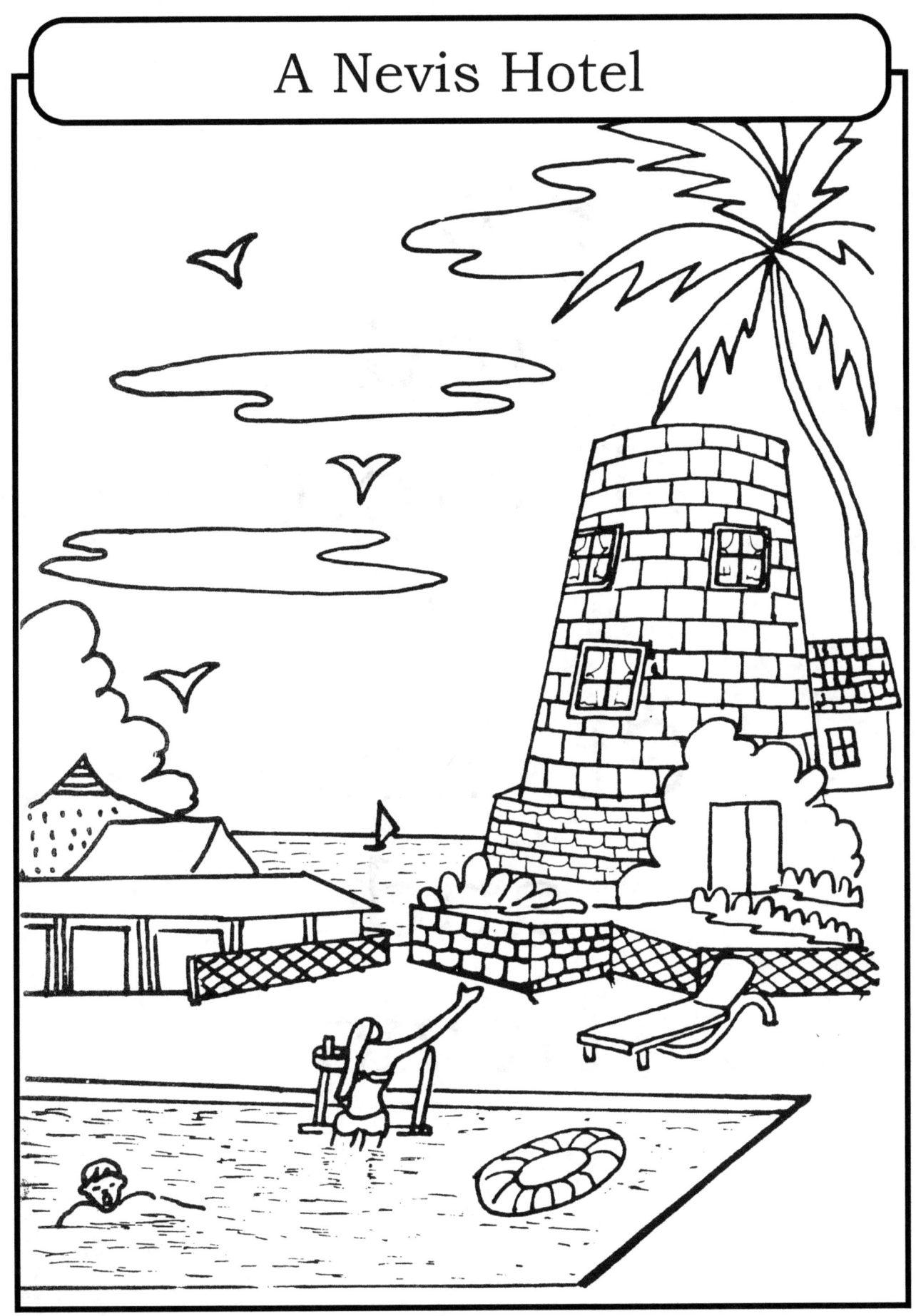

Flora
and
Fauna
of
St. Kitts
and
Nevis

Poinciana

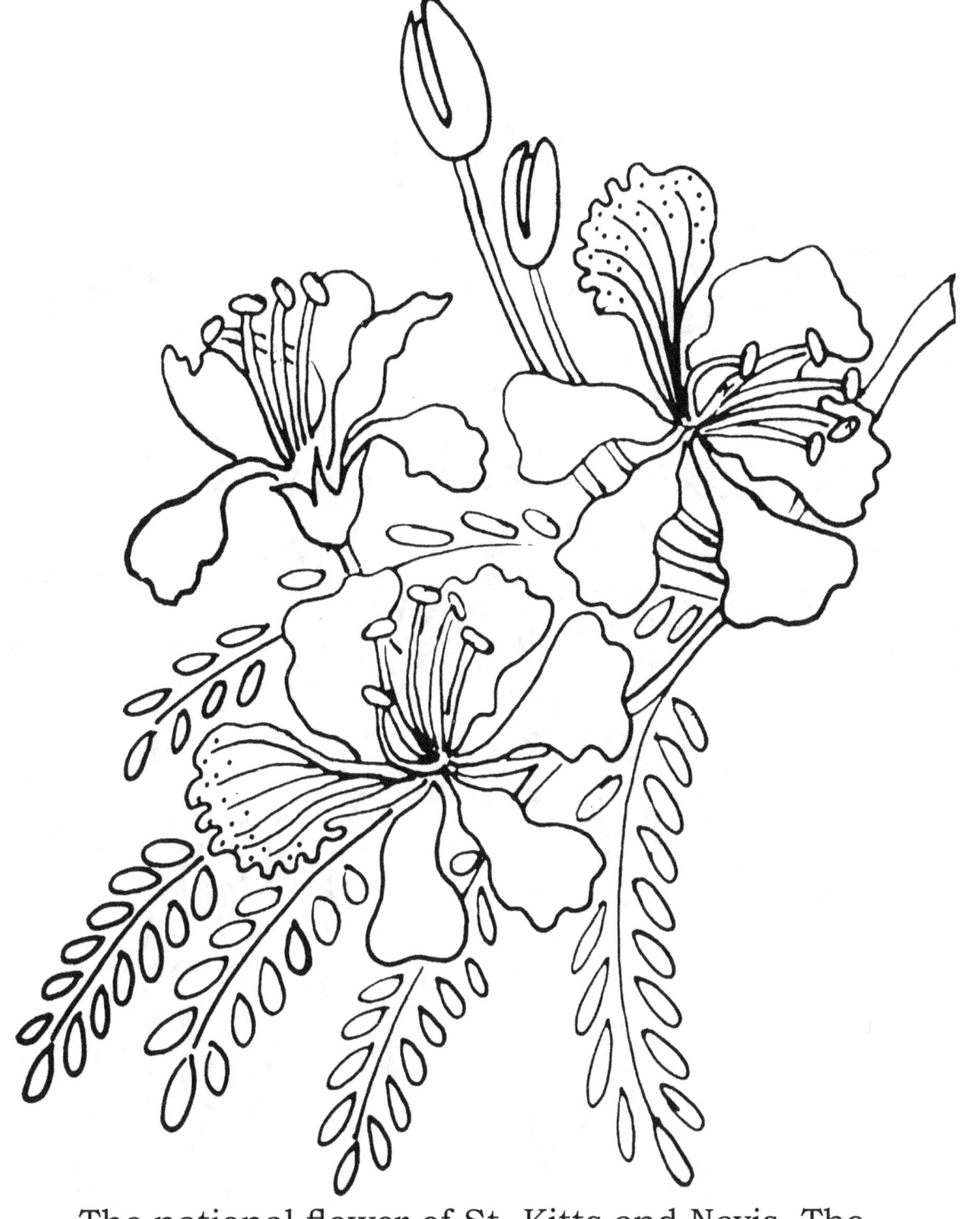

The national flower of St. Kitts and Nevis. The tree was brought to the islands by Governor De Poincy, the first French Governor, around 1787.

Banana Tree

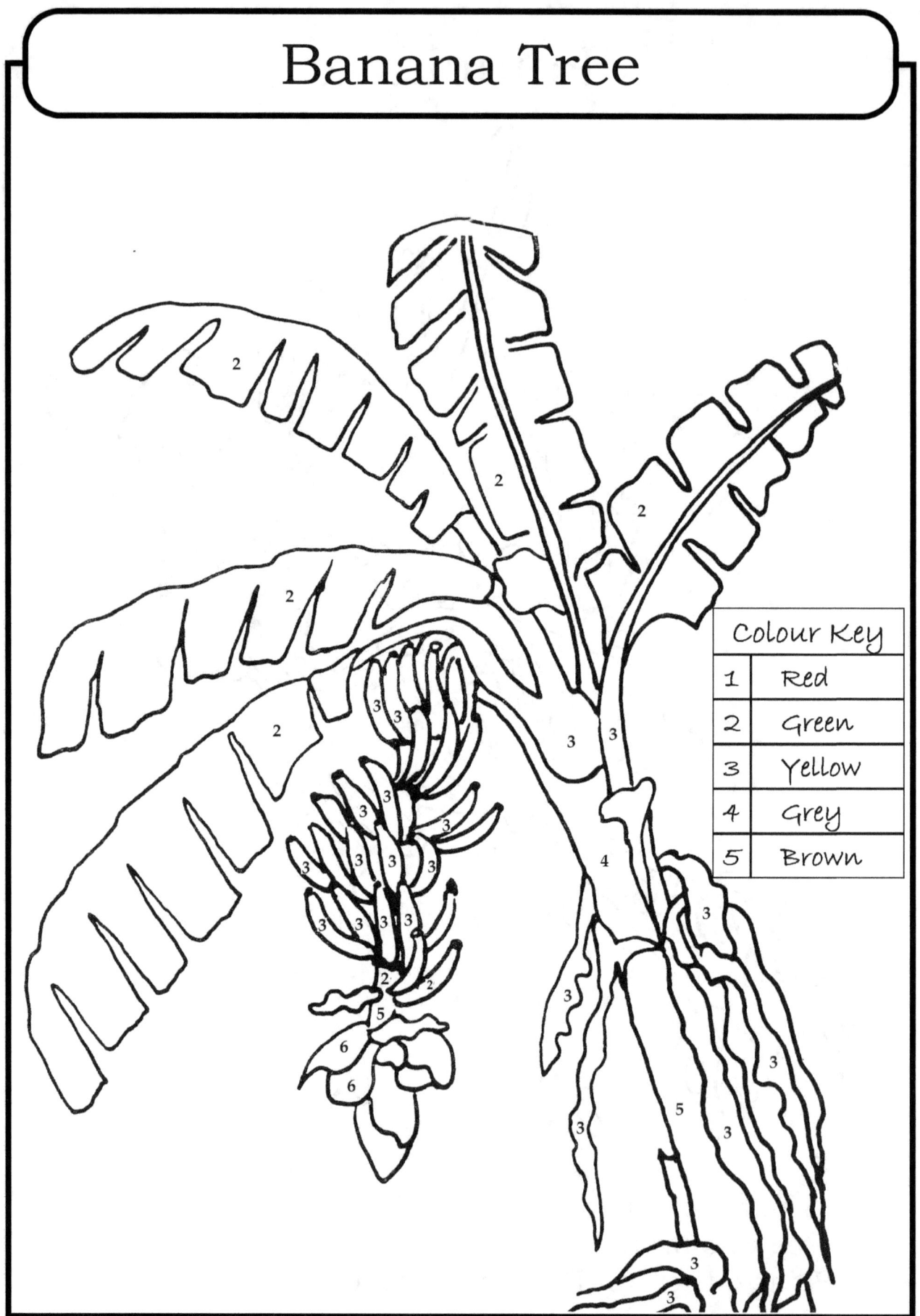

Colour Key	
1	Red
2	Green
3	Yellow
4	Grey
5	Brown

Tropical Fruit

Can you name these fruit?
They are all found in St. Kitts and Nevis.

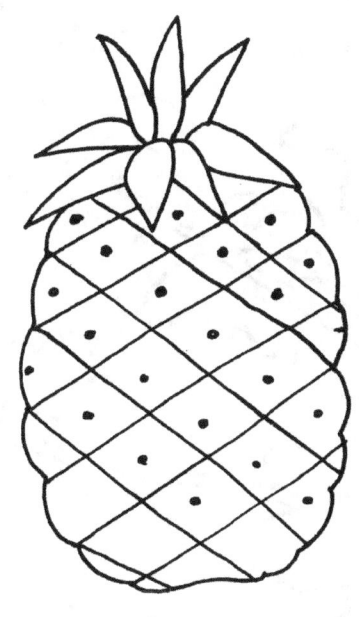

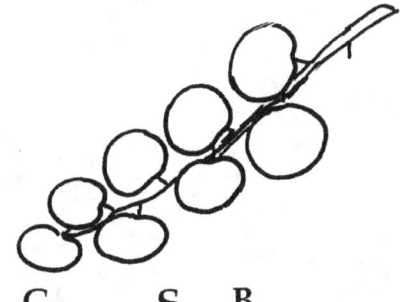

G _ _ _ S _ B _ _ _ Y

P _ _ _ _ _ P P _ _

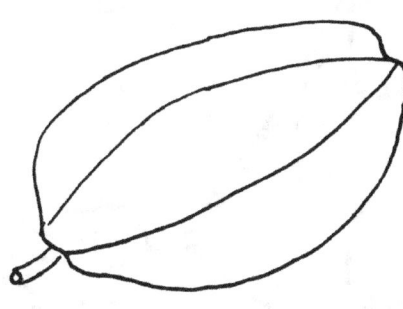

P _ _ _ P _ _

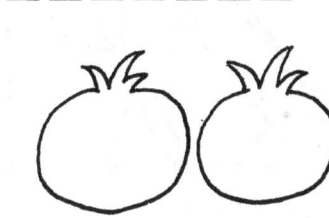

_ _ _ G _ _ S

G _ _ _ _ _ S

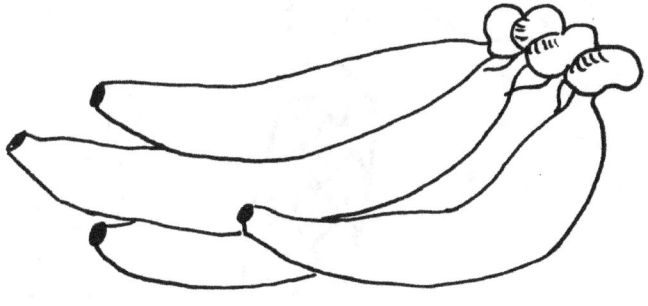

B _ _ _ _ _ S

Pawpaw Tree

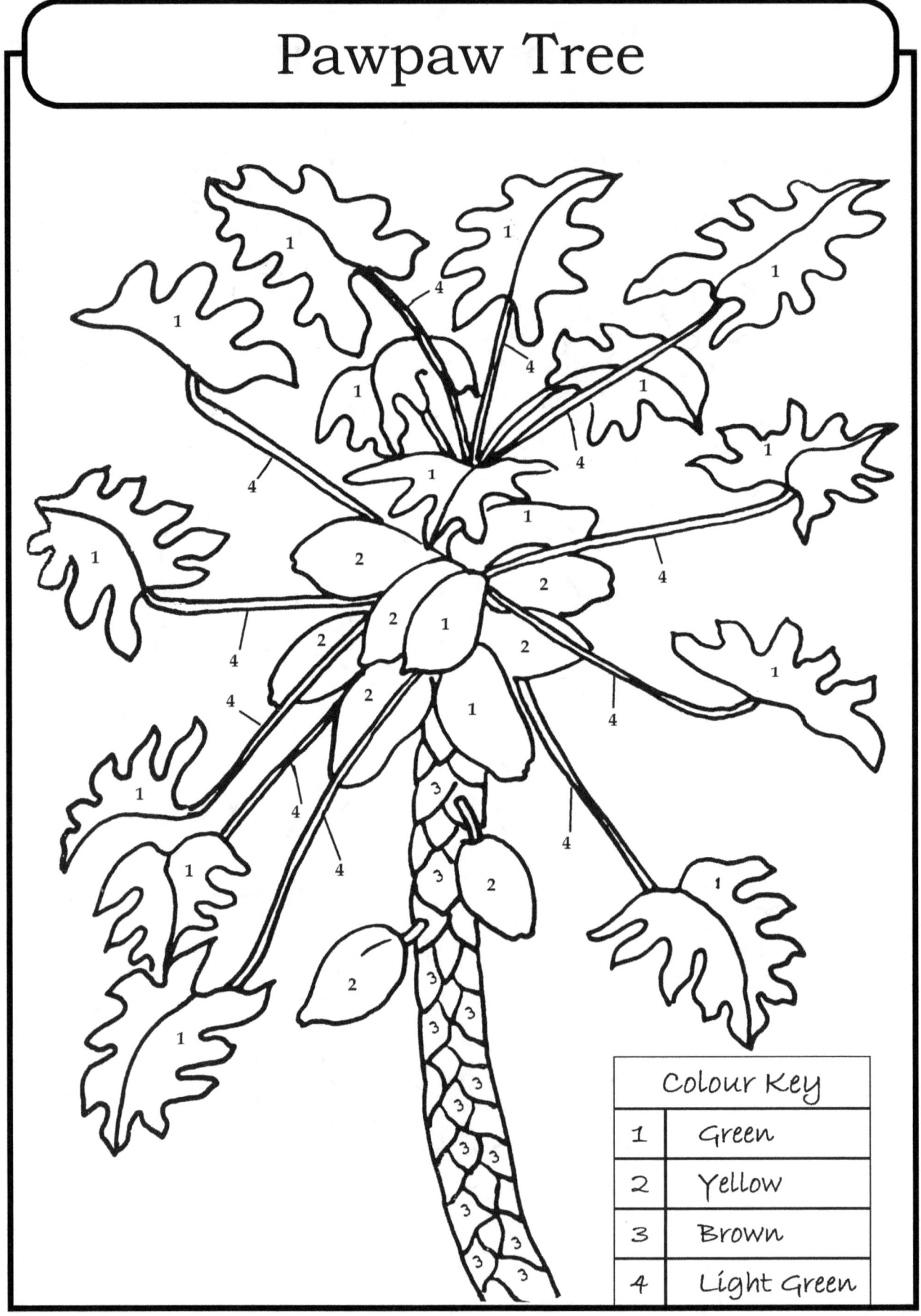

Colour Key	
1	Green
2	Yellow
3	Brown
4	Light Green

Flowers of St. Kitts and Nevis

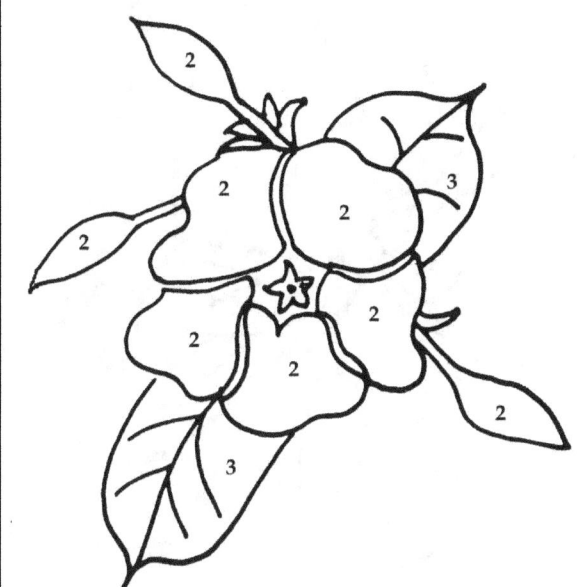

Alamanda or Yellow Bell

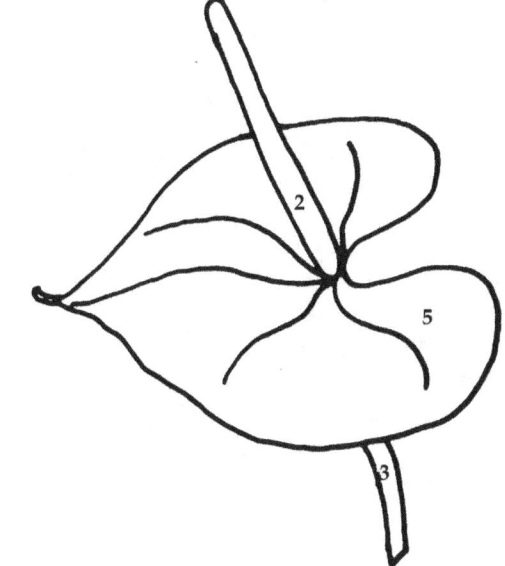

Anthurium

Red Ginger
Lily

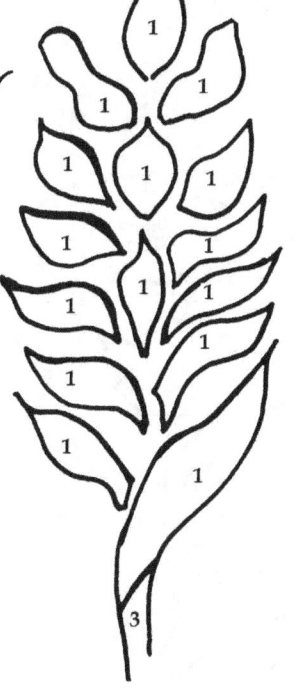

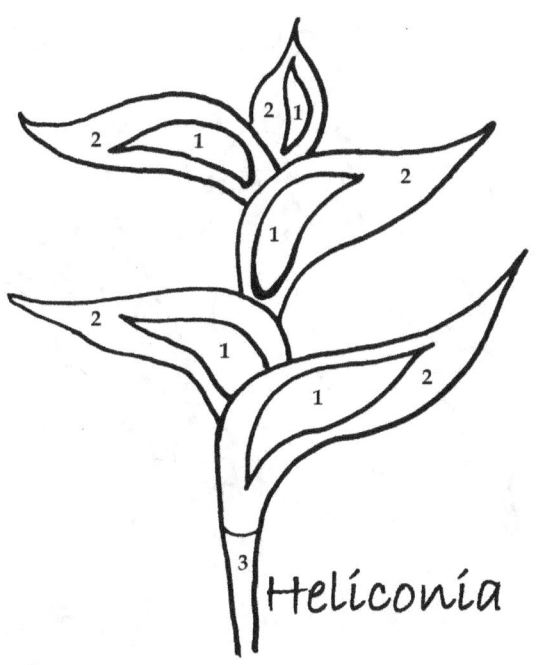

Heliconia

Colour Key	
1	Red
2	Yellow
3	Green
4	Brown
5	Pink

Tropical Butterflies

Large Orange Sulphur

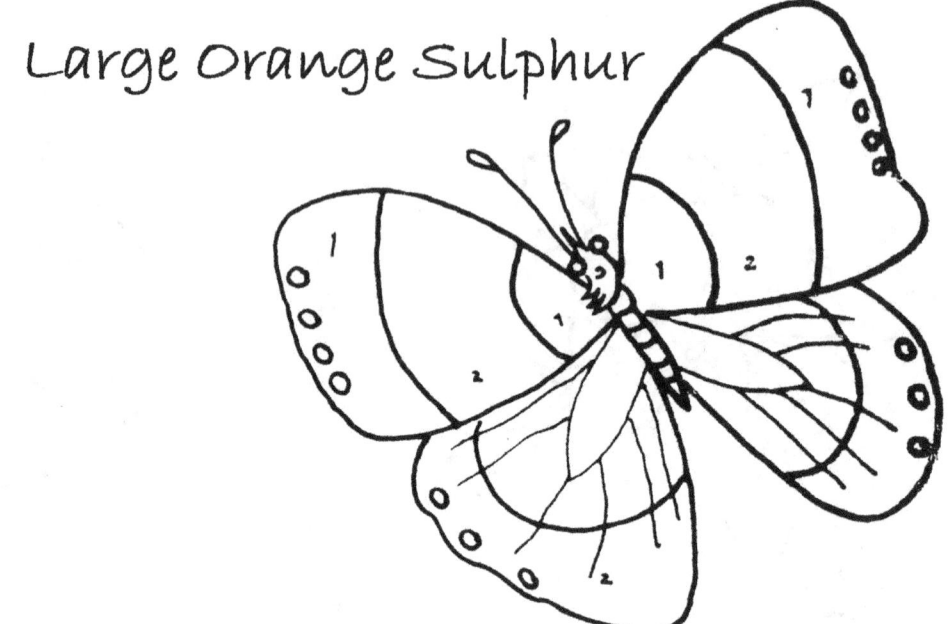

Malachite

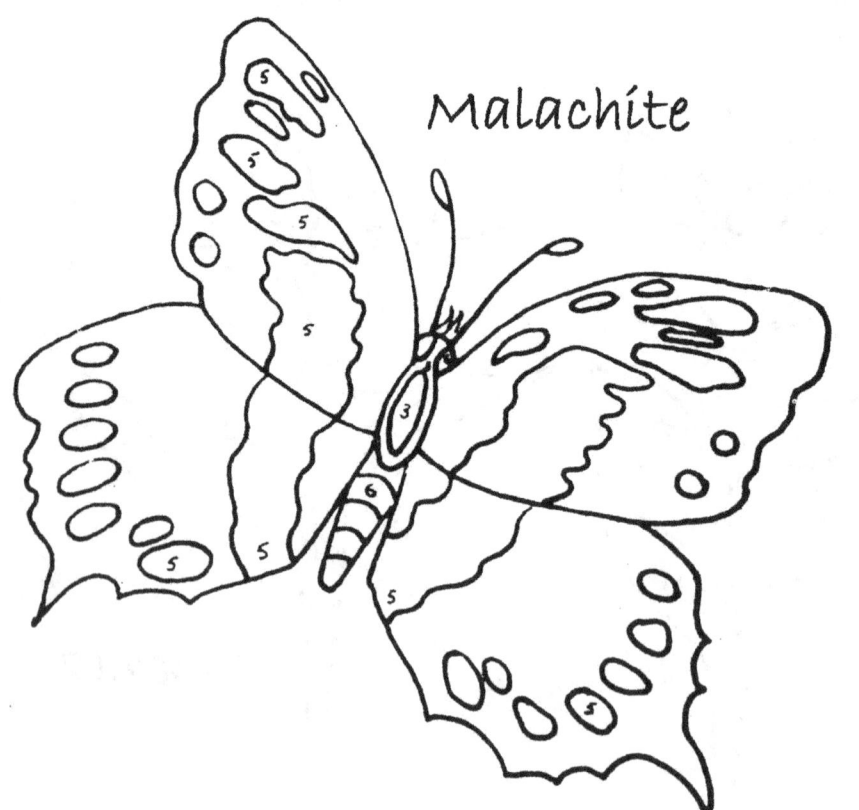

Colour Key	
1	Yellow
2	Orange
3	Black
4	Red
5	White
6	Light Brown

Vervet Monkeys

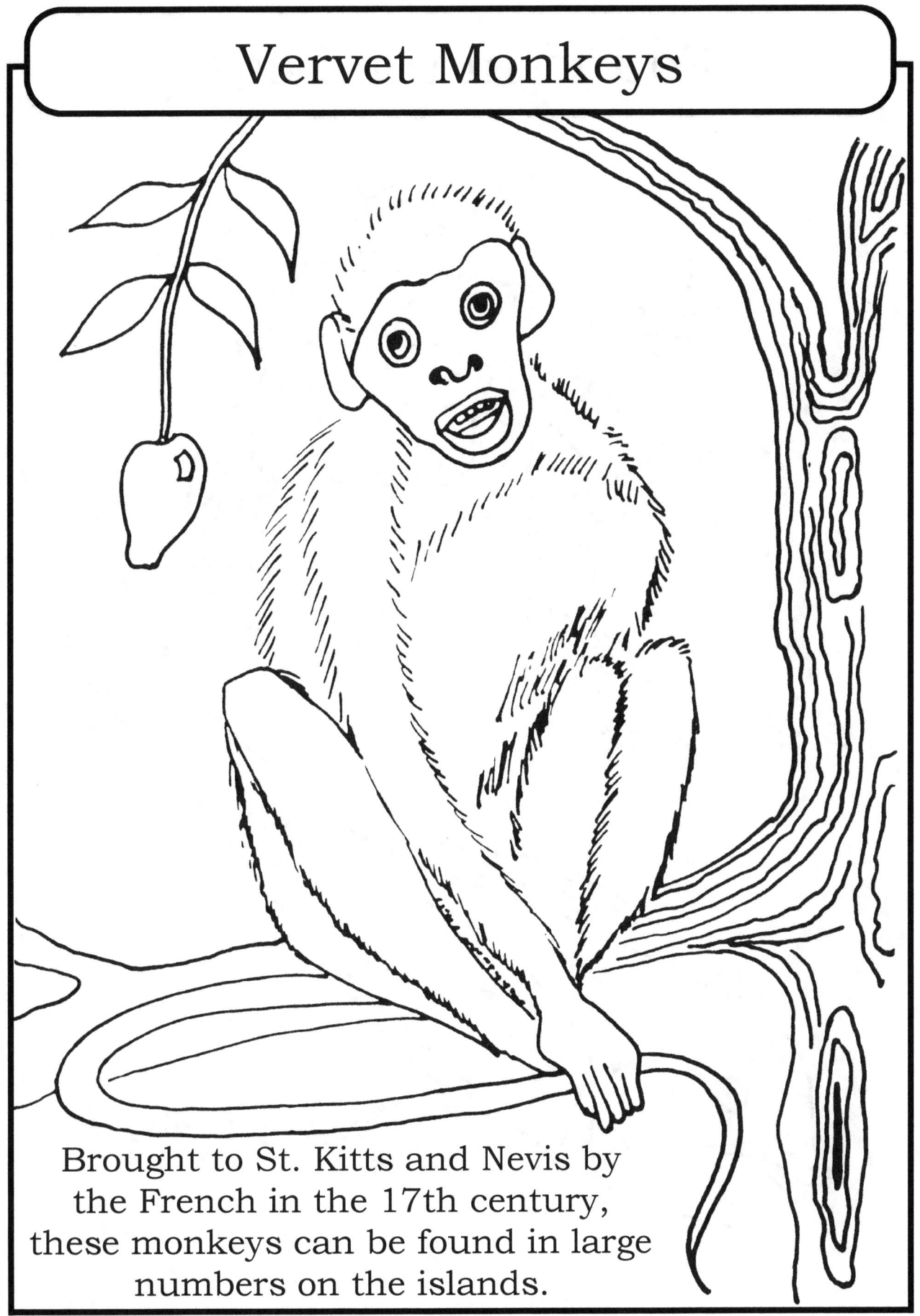

Brought to St. Kitts and Nevis by
the French in the 17th century,
these monkeys can be found in large
numbers on the islands.

Found in the Seas

Green Turtle

Mahi-Mahi

Spiny Lobster

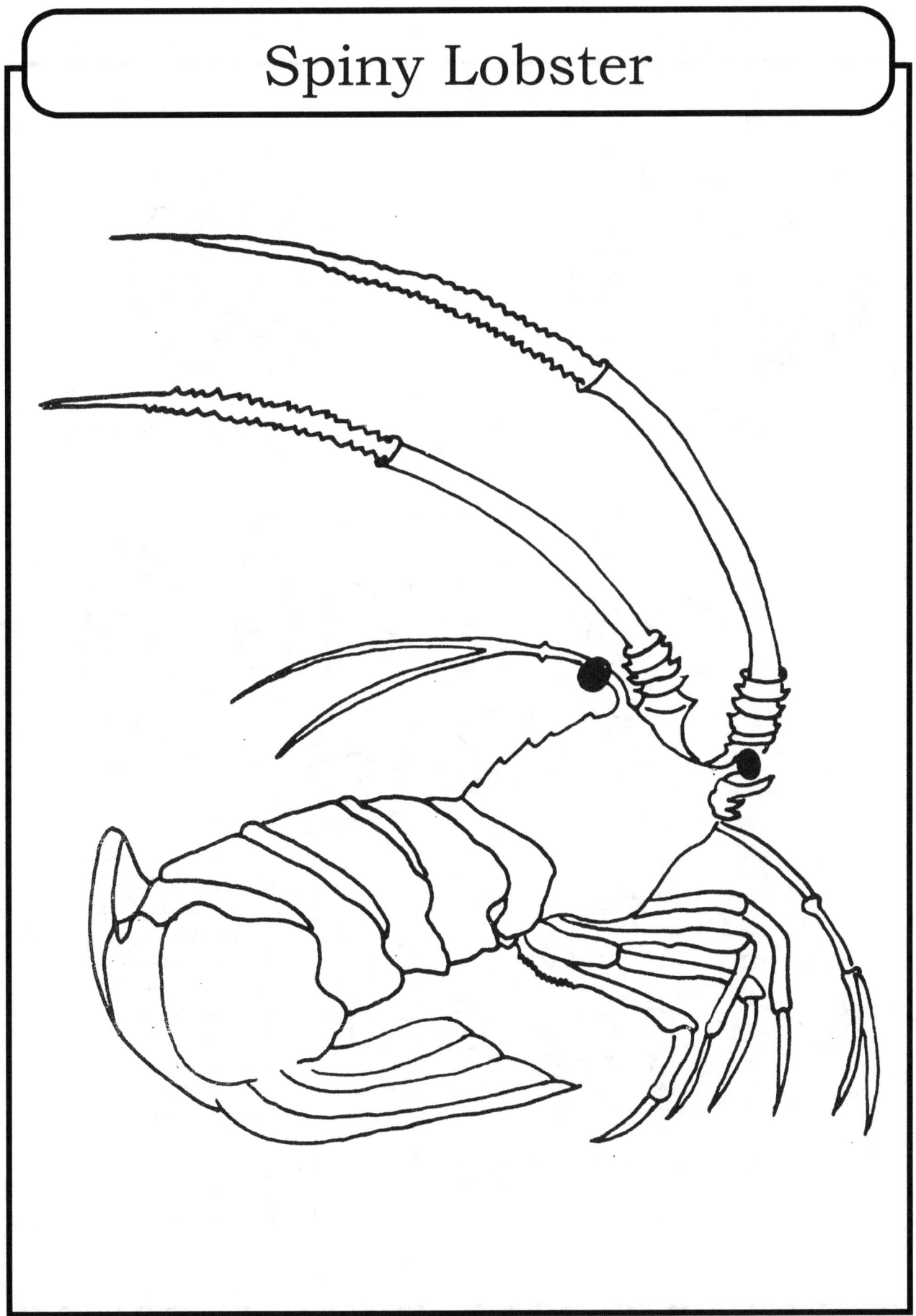

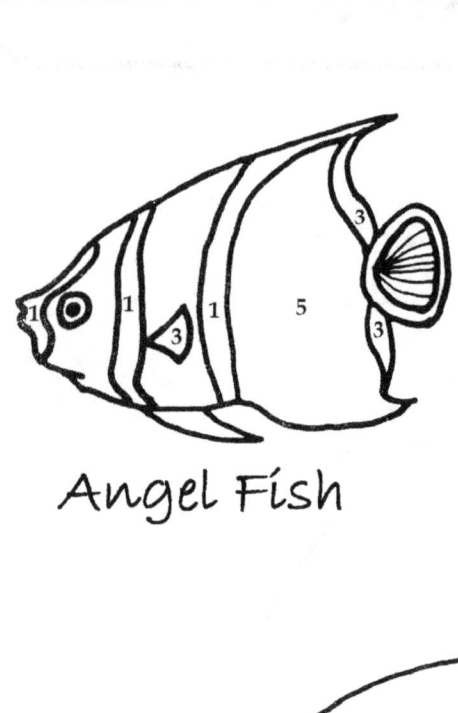

Angel Fish

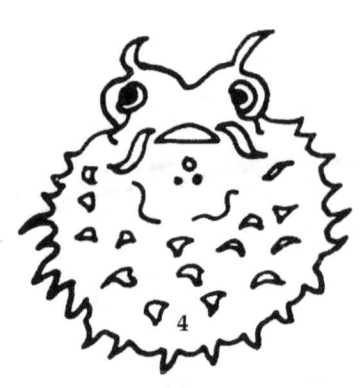

Spiny Puffer

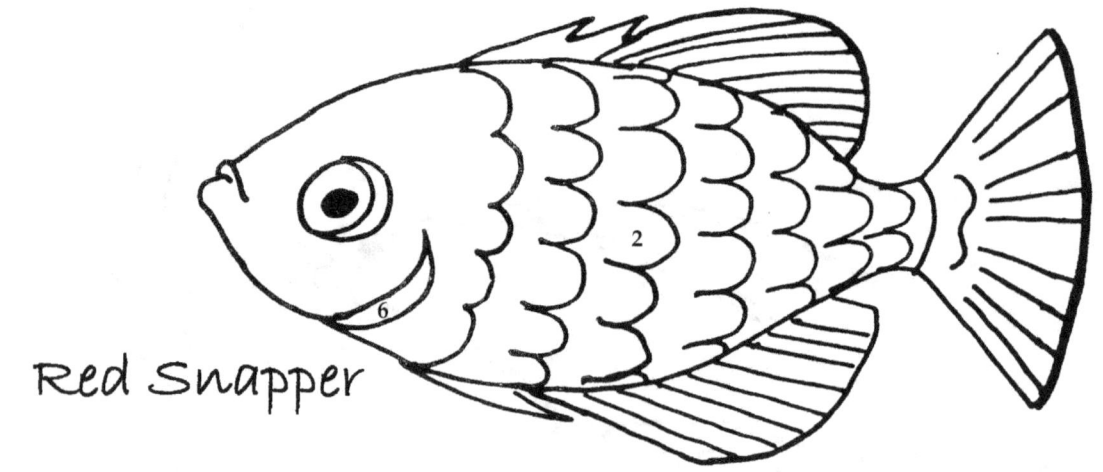

Red Snapper

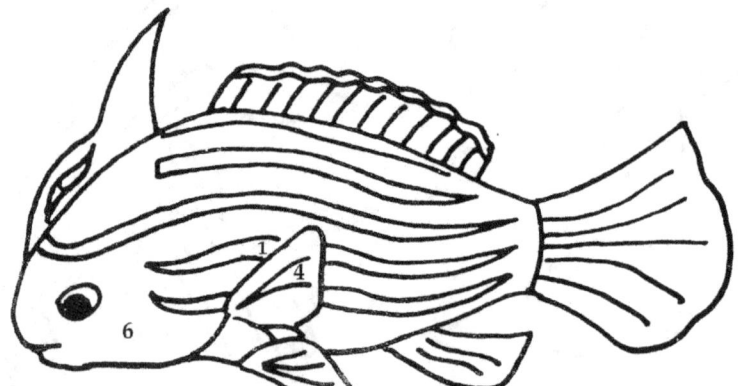

High Hat (Cubbyu)

Colour Key	
1	White
2	Red
3	Blue
4	Yellow
5	Black
6	Brown

28

Donkeys

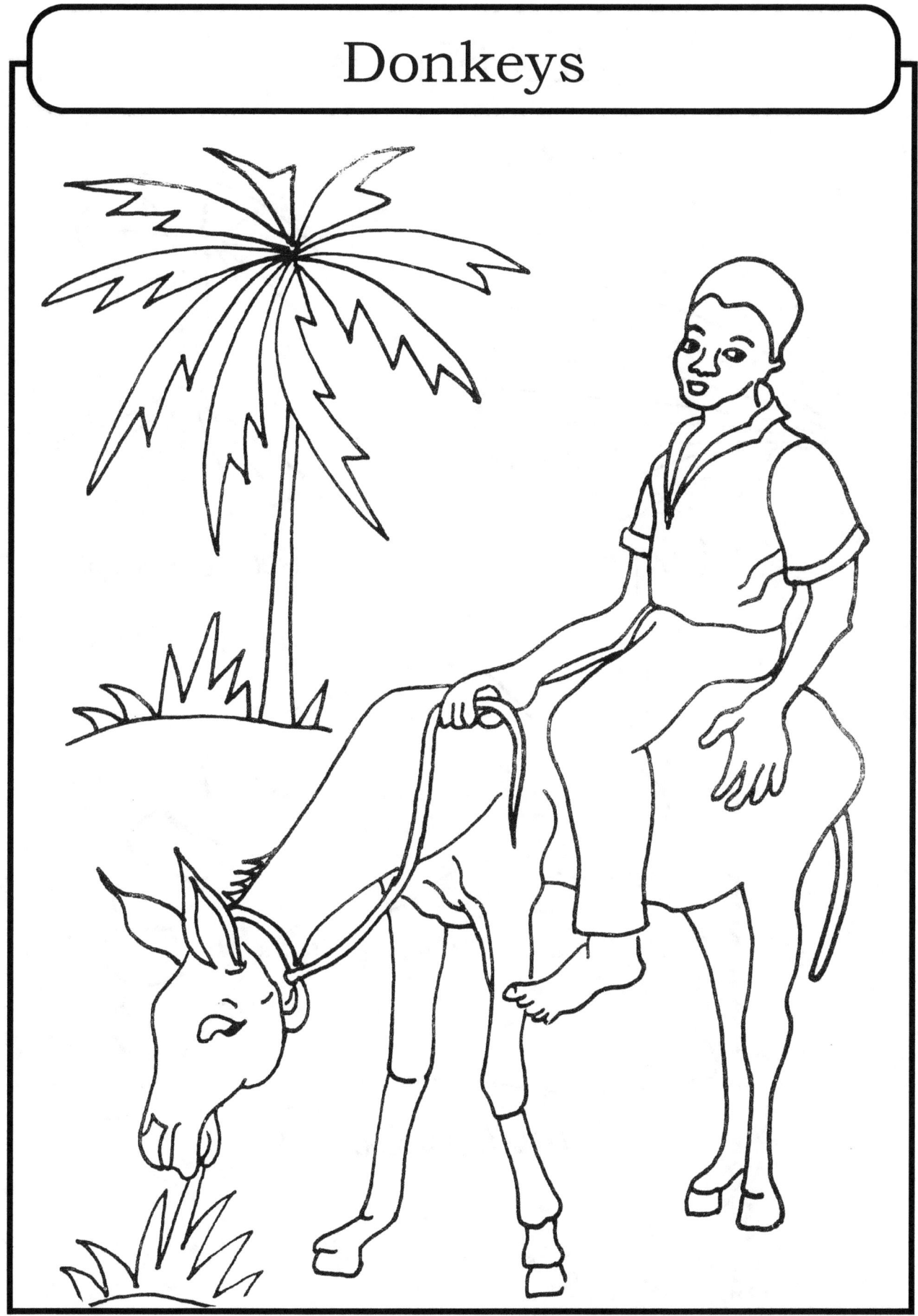

Sea Shells

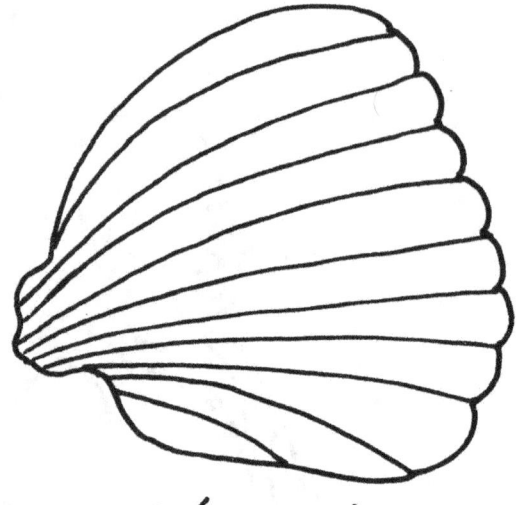

Limpet

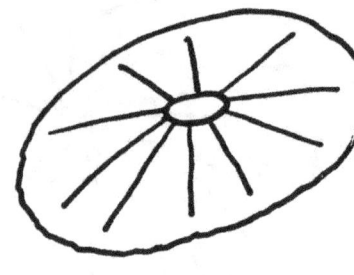

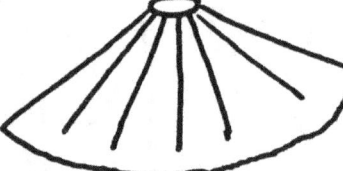

Rose Cups

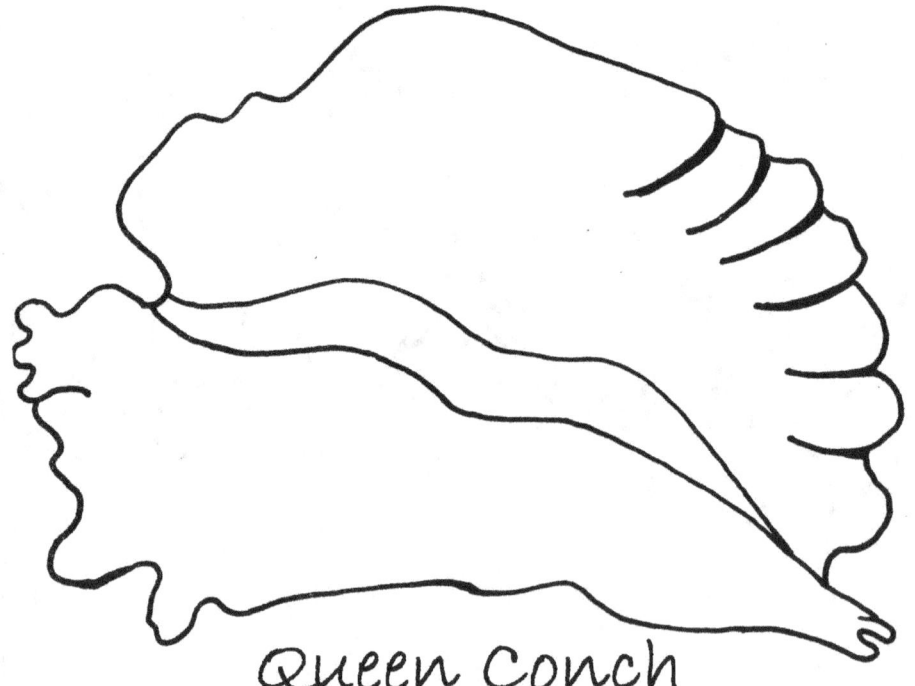

Queen Conch

Tropical Word Search

M	M	O	A	R	C	D	R	W	Z	Y	P	R	A	T	N	I	C	F	A
U	A	G	P	O	D	D	G	M	G	G	L	O	E	I	U	K	X	I	E
I	H	N	D	I	H	X	A	V	C	Q	W	F	I	P	X	R	N	S	Z
R	I	A	Y	S	L	L	E	H	S	A	E	S	R	N	P	O	T	H	P
U	M	M	B	S	A	G	D	R	E	A	P	N	B	E	C	A	P	L	E
H	A	L	M	C	W	T	S	S	E	K	N	W	N	I	T	I	N	N	E
T	H	S	H	V	C	K	O	D	P	F	W	G	L	K	F	T	A	S	I
N	I	I	B	A	N	A	N	A	I	W	F	E	E	A	L	L	U	N	O
A	T	Q	U	P	J	R	L	Z	N	A	H	U	Y	L	O	U	F	B	A
E	T	A	H	H	G	I	H	V	E	P	Q	A	P	B	W	Z	H	V	L
A	L	A	M	A	N	D	E	R	A	W	P	O	S	P	E	O	A	I	G
K	V	V	Z	E	X	R	M	I	P	A	G	T	N	D	R	U	L	A	P
T	R	E	E	S	V	T	G	Y	P	P	E	M	K	P	G	Y	W	Q	C
F	J	Q	Z	E	Z	T	K	F	L	R	Y	E	K	N	O	M	F	S	Y
I	T	V	T	S	B	X	M	O	E	J	K	Y	R	T	K	W	E	O	E

Word List

ALAMANDER	GUAVA	MANGO	SEASHELLS
ANGEL	HELICONIA	MONKEY	SNAPPER
ANTHURIUM	HIGH HAT	PAPAYA	TREES
BANANA	LILY	PAWPAW	TURTLE
BUTTERFLY	LOBSTER	PINEAPPLE	VERVET
FISH	MAHI MAHI	POINCIANA	
FLOWER	MALACHITE	PUFFER	

Popular Activities in St. Kitts and Nevis

Cricket

One of the most popular sports in St. Kitts and Nevis.

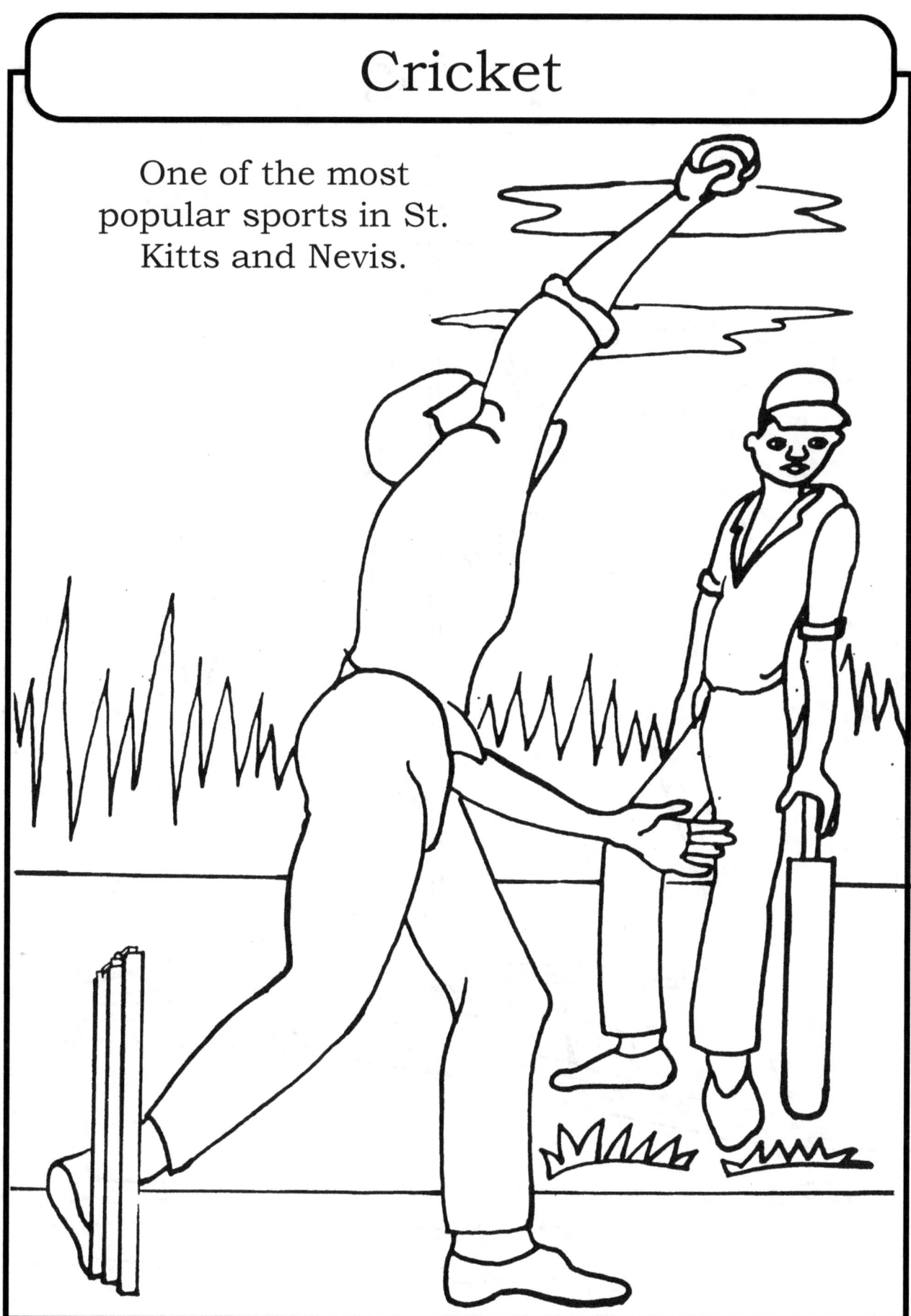

Sailing

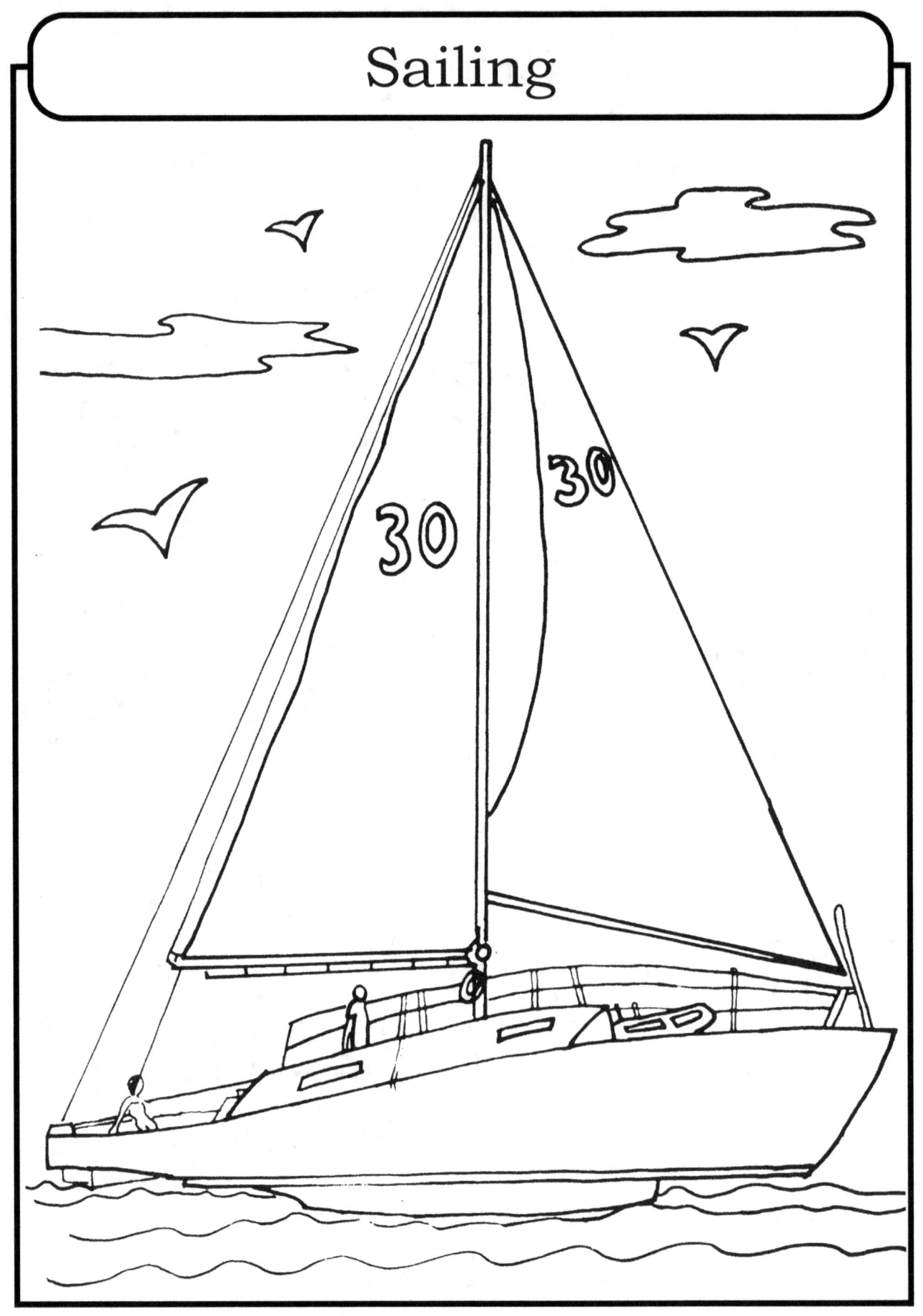

Football

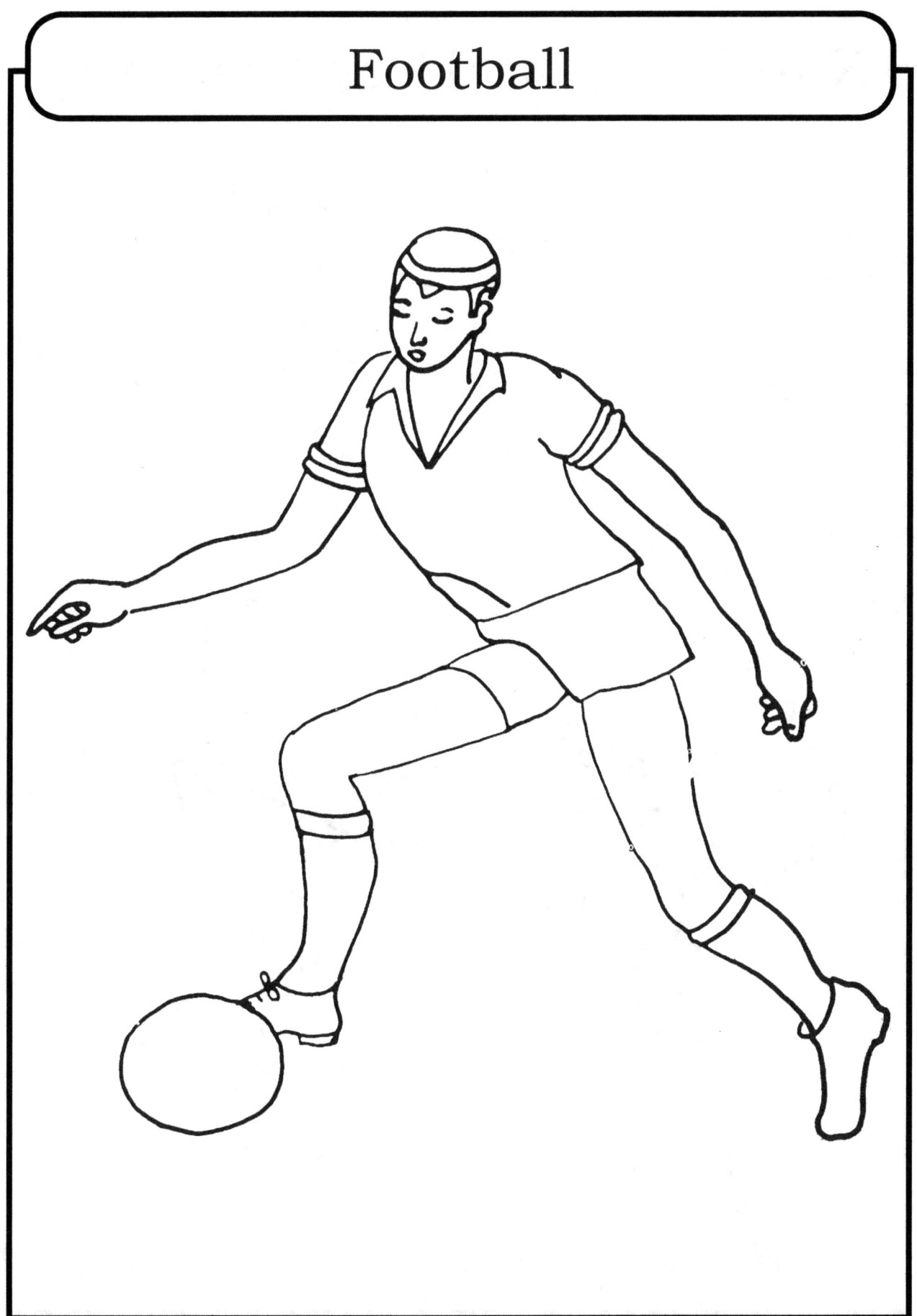

Kite Flying and Top Spinning

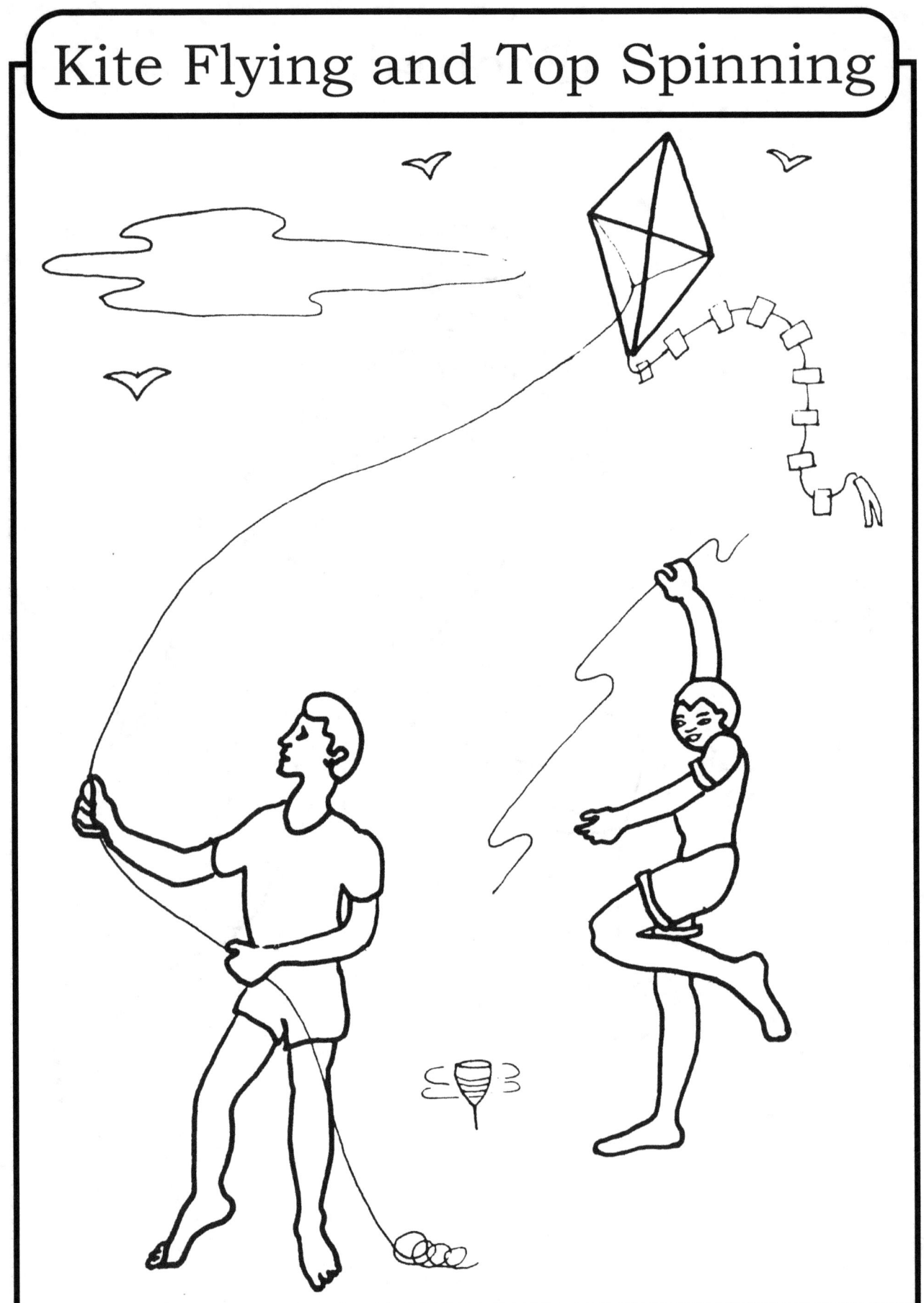

Golf

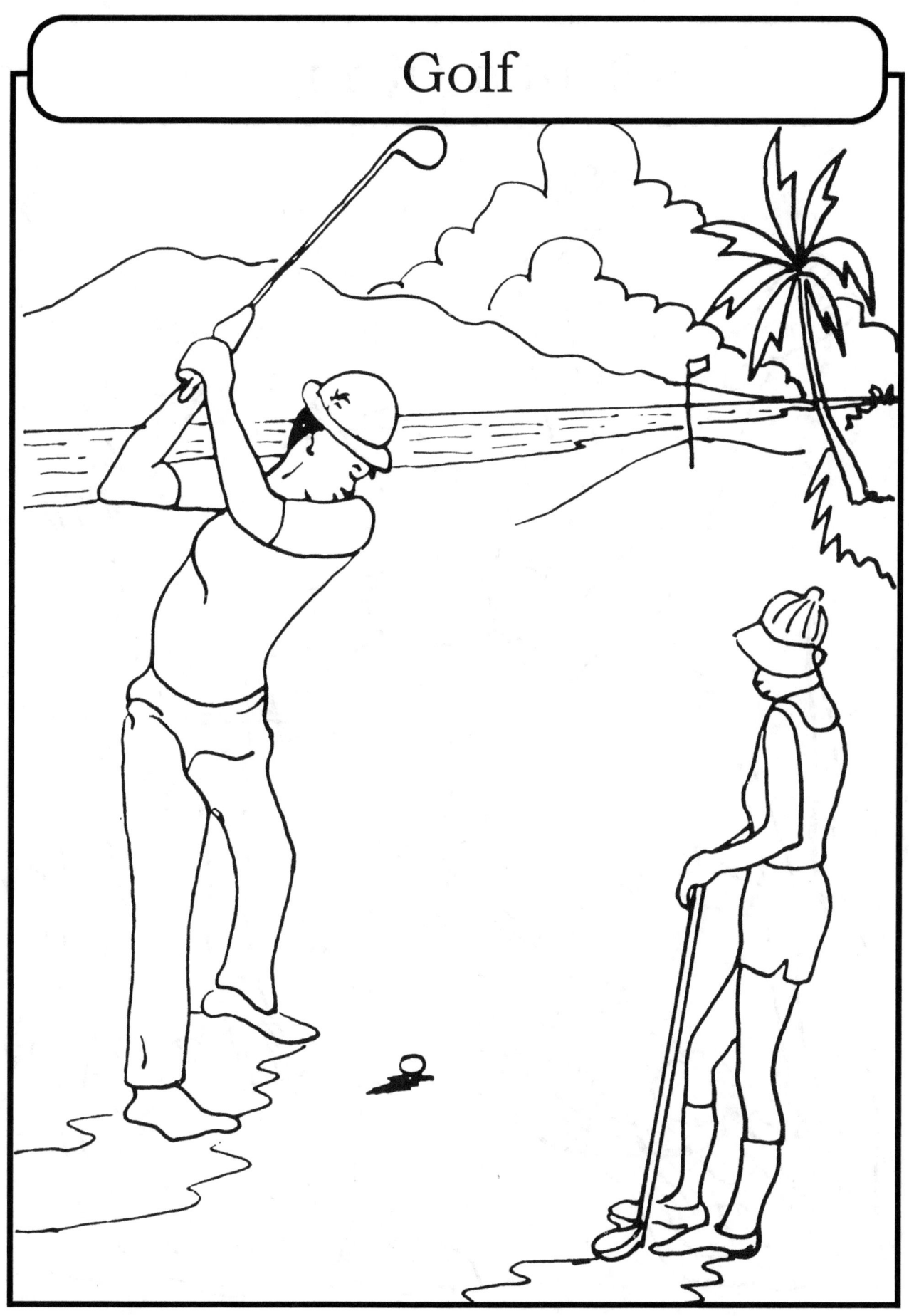

Scuba Diving

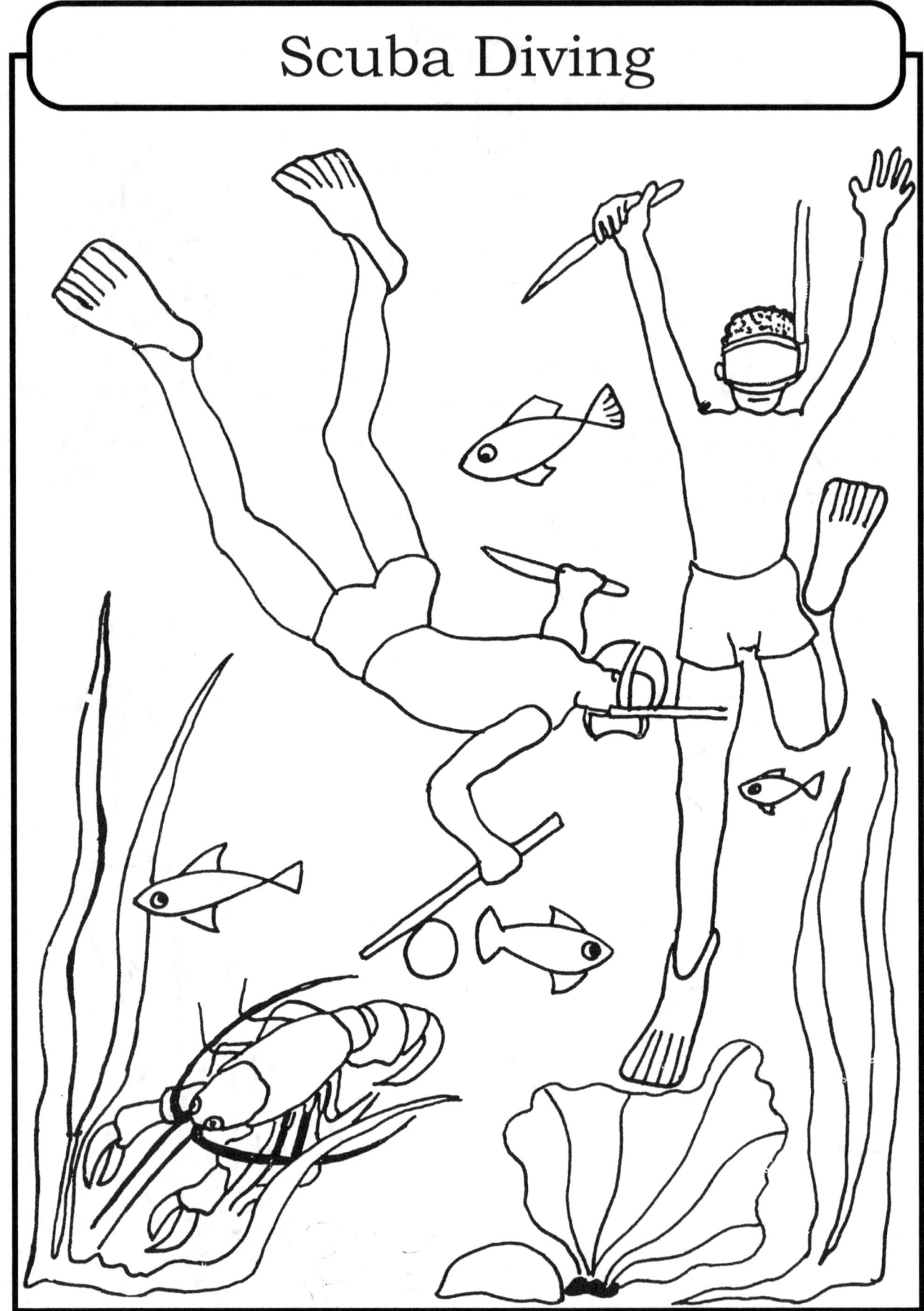

Dining Out

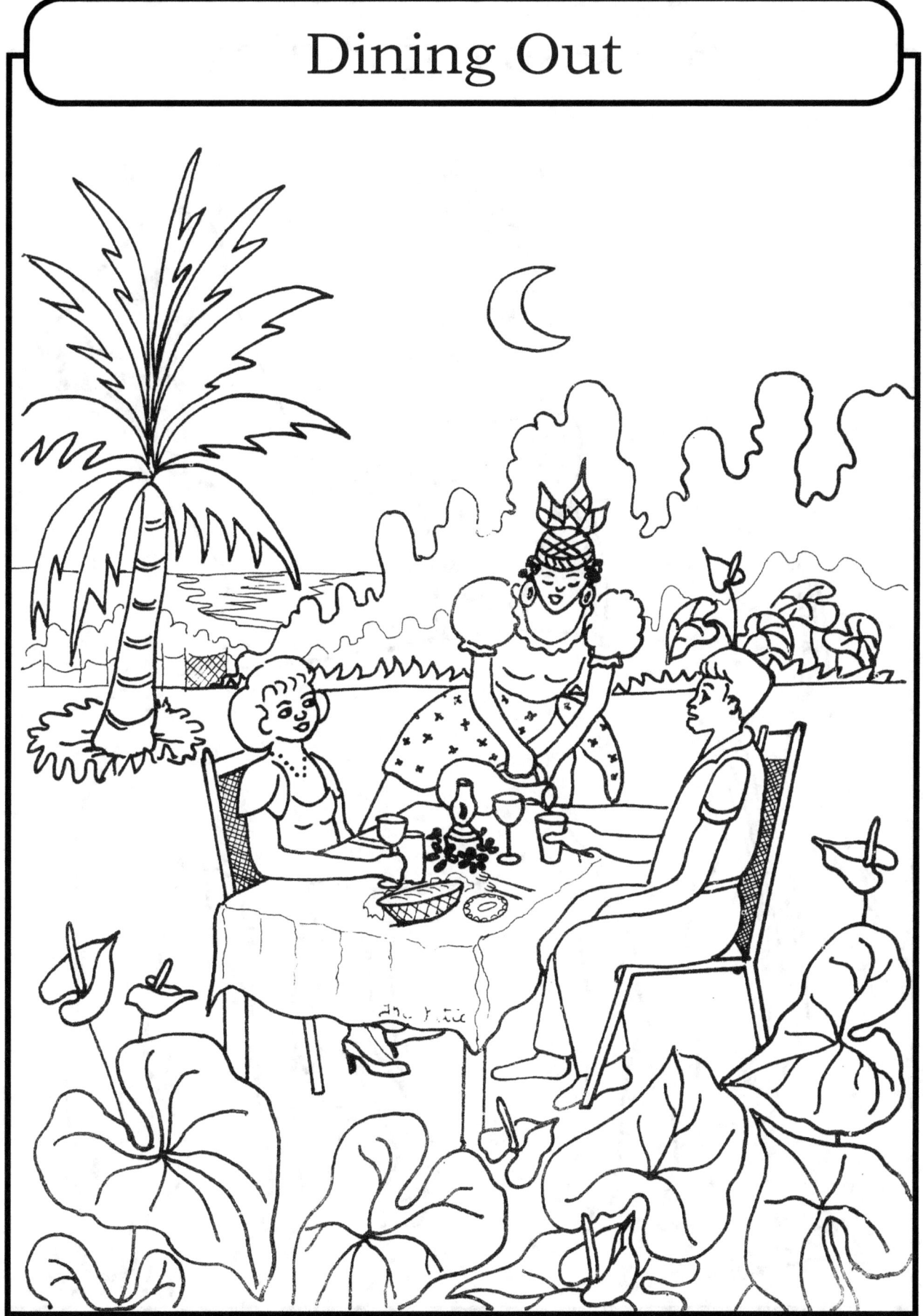

Horse-back Riding

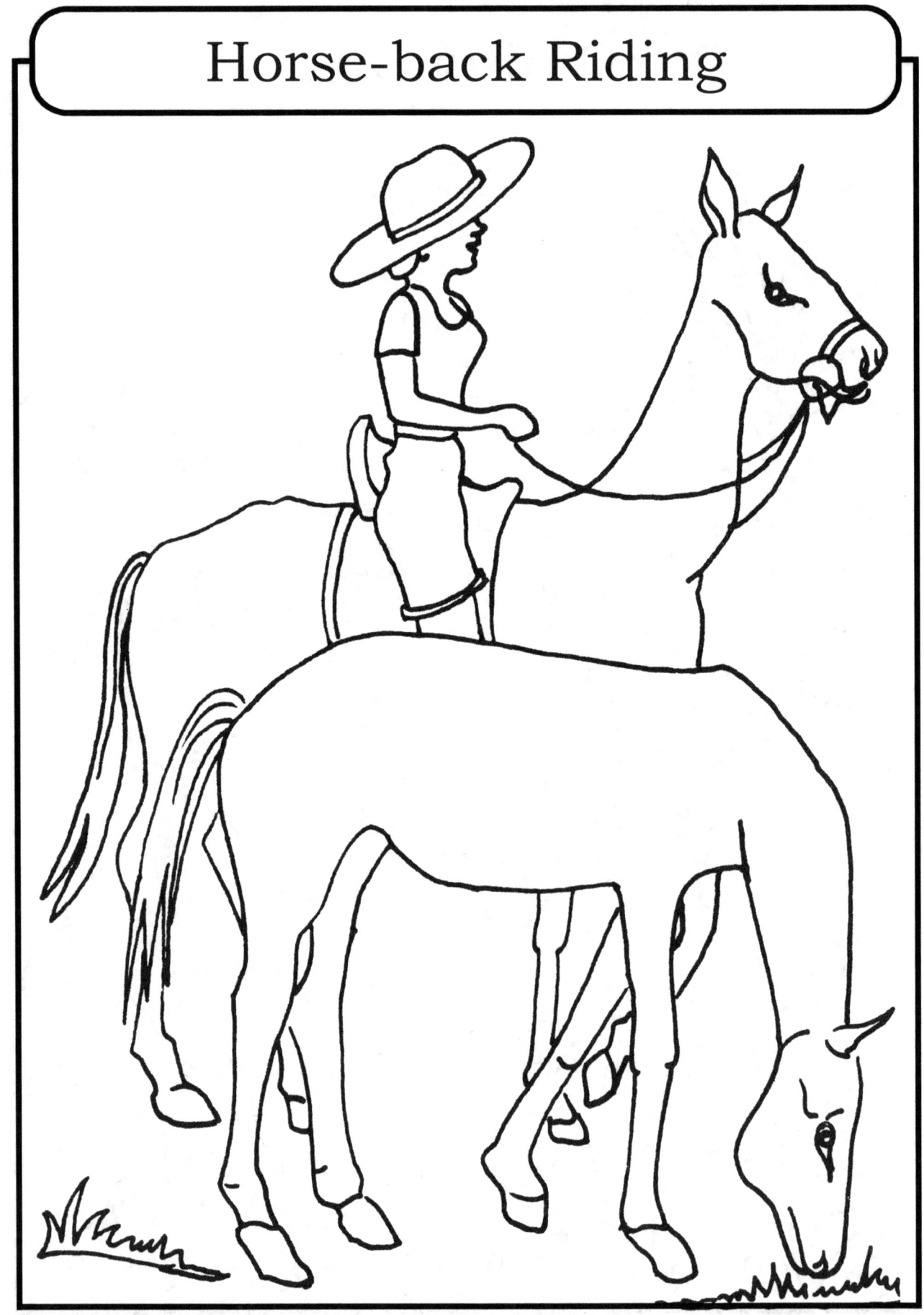

Ziplining

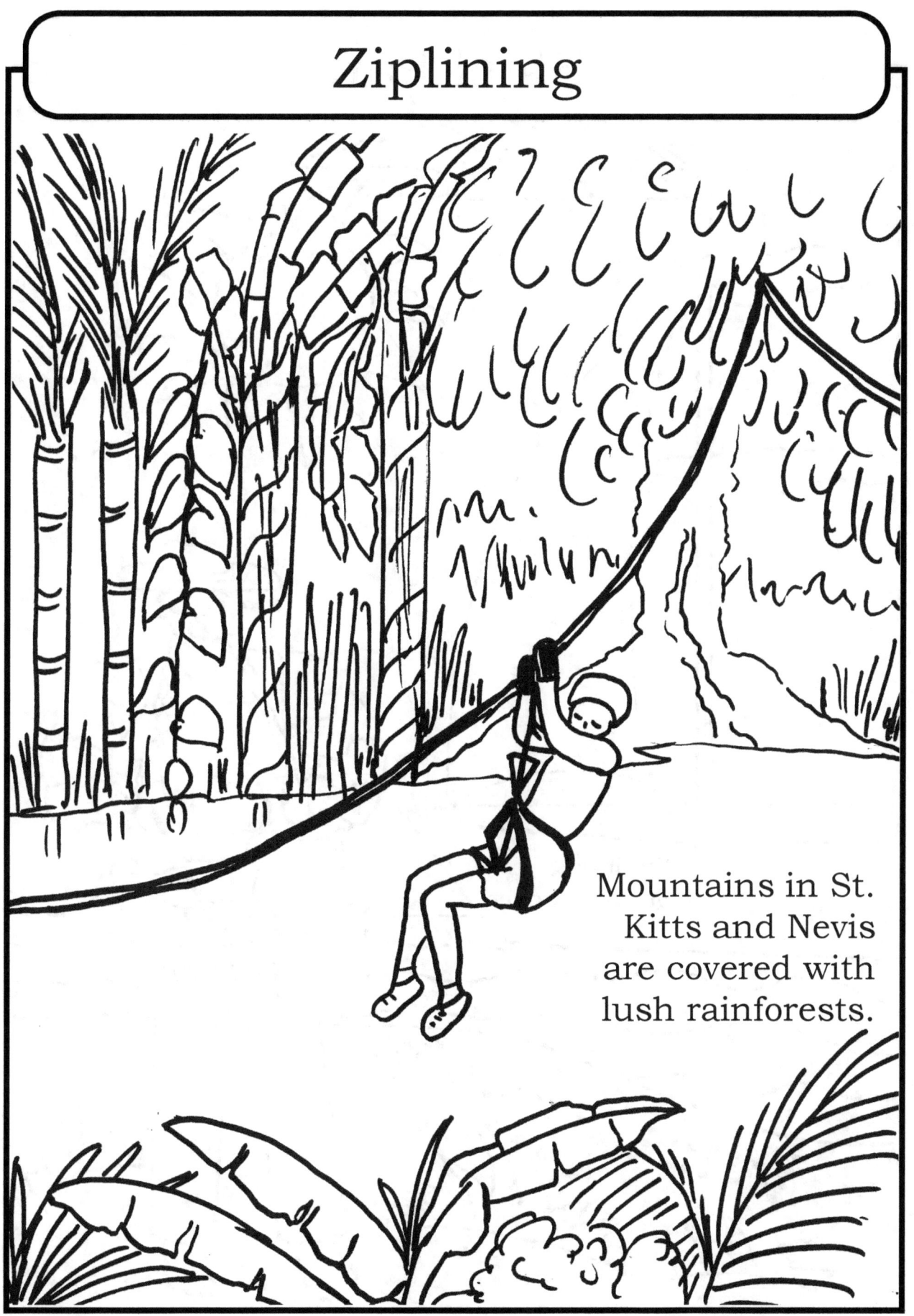

Mountains in St. Kitts and Nevis are covered with lush rainforests.

Steel Pan

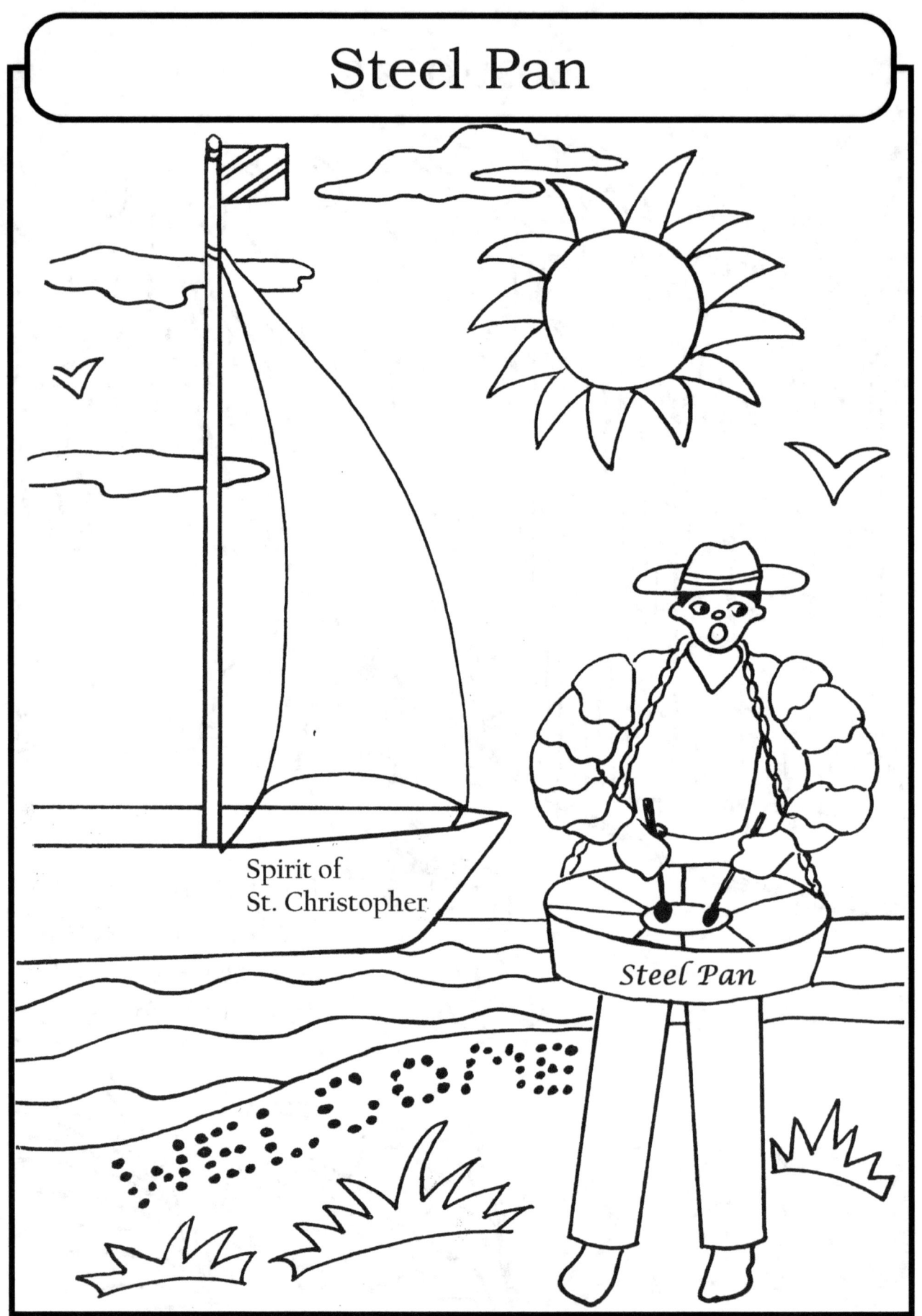

Spirit of
St. Christopher

Steel Pan

WELCOME

Places
and
People
of interest in
St. Kitts
and
Nevis

Black Rocks

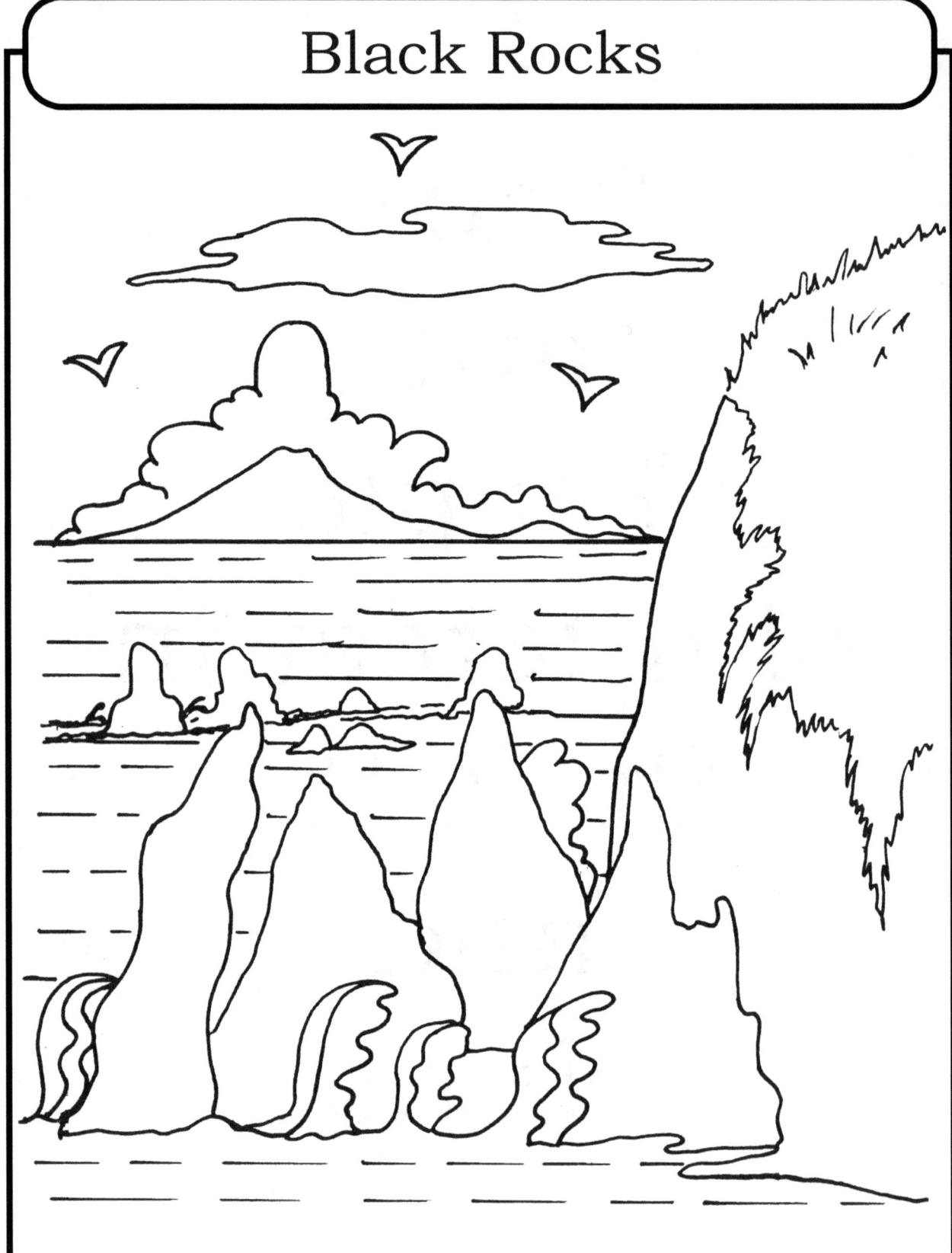

These majestic black volcanic rocks were formed millions of years ago from lava flow from Mount Liamuiga.

Caribelle Batik

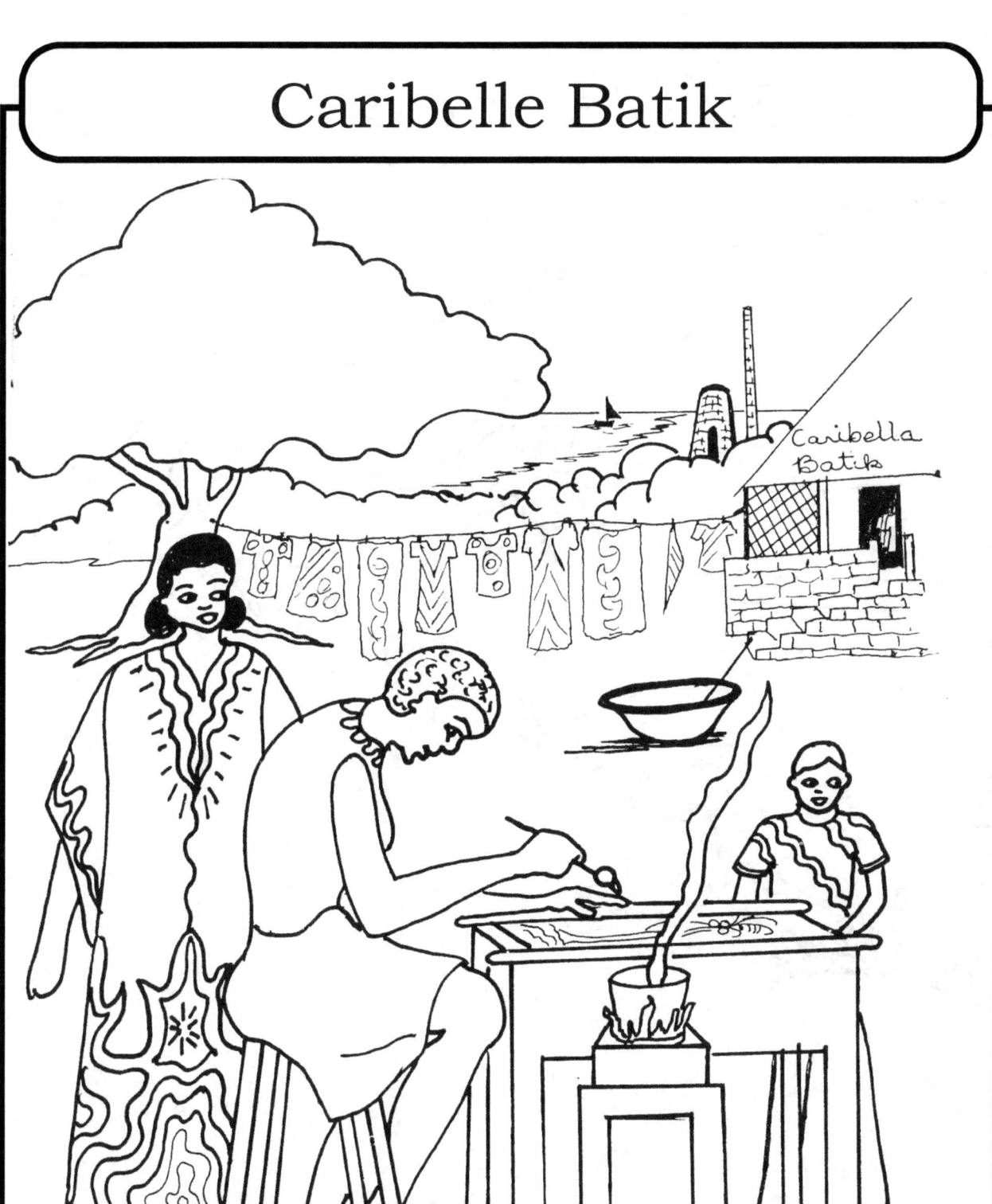

Designers use wax and dye to create brightly
coloured patterns on fabric.

Frigate Bay Beach

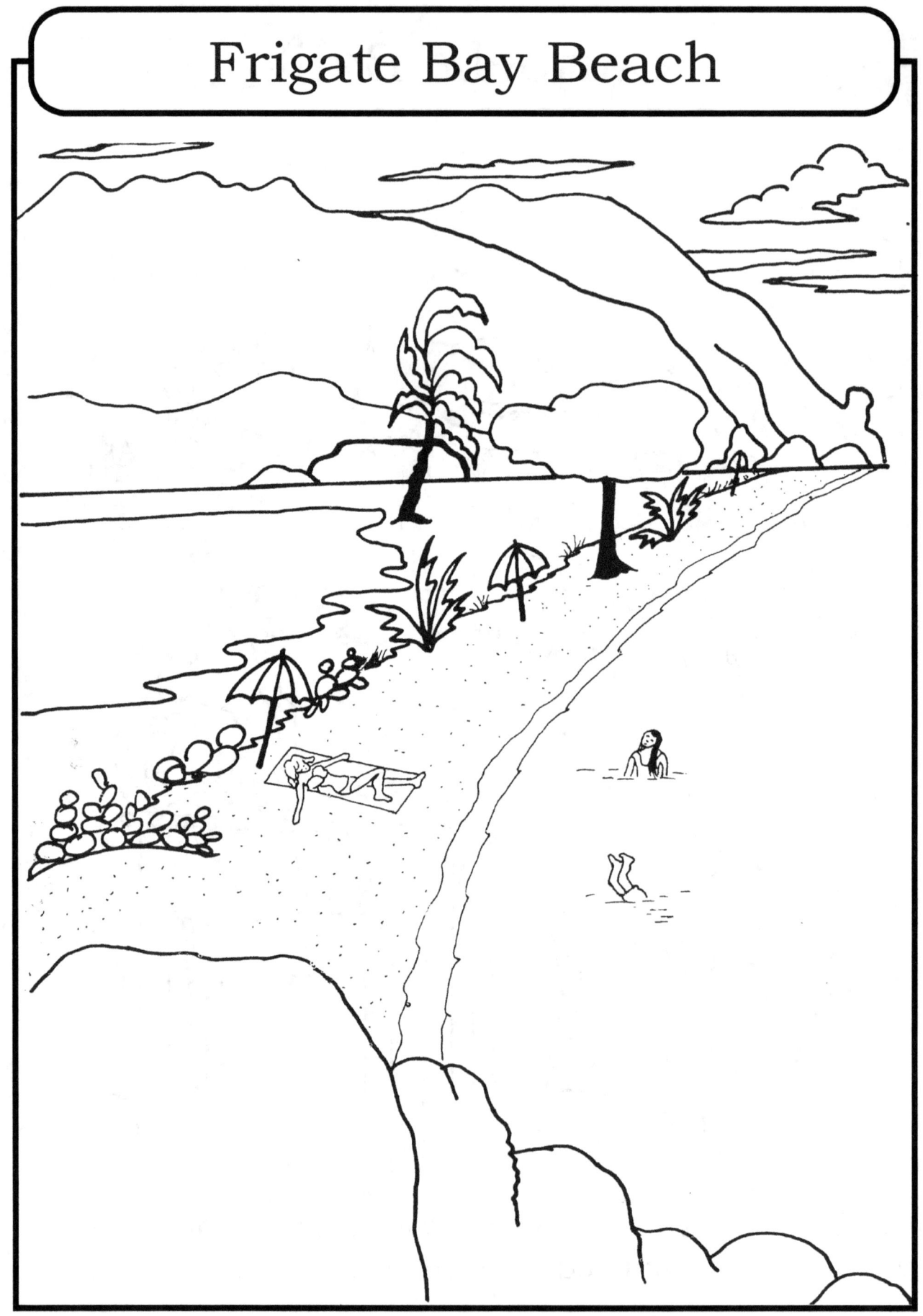

Boat Building

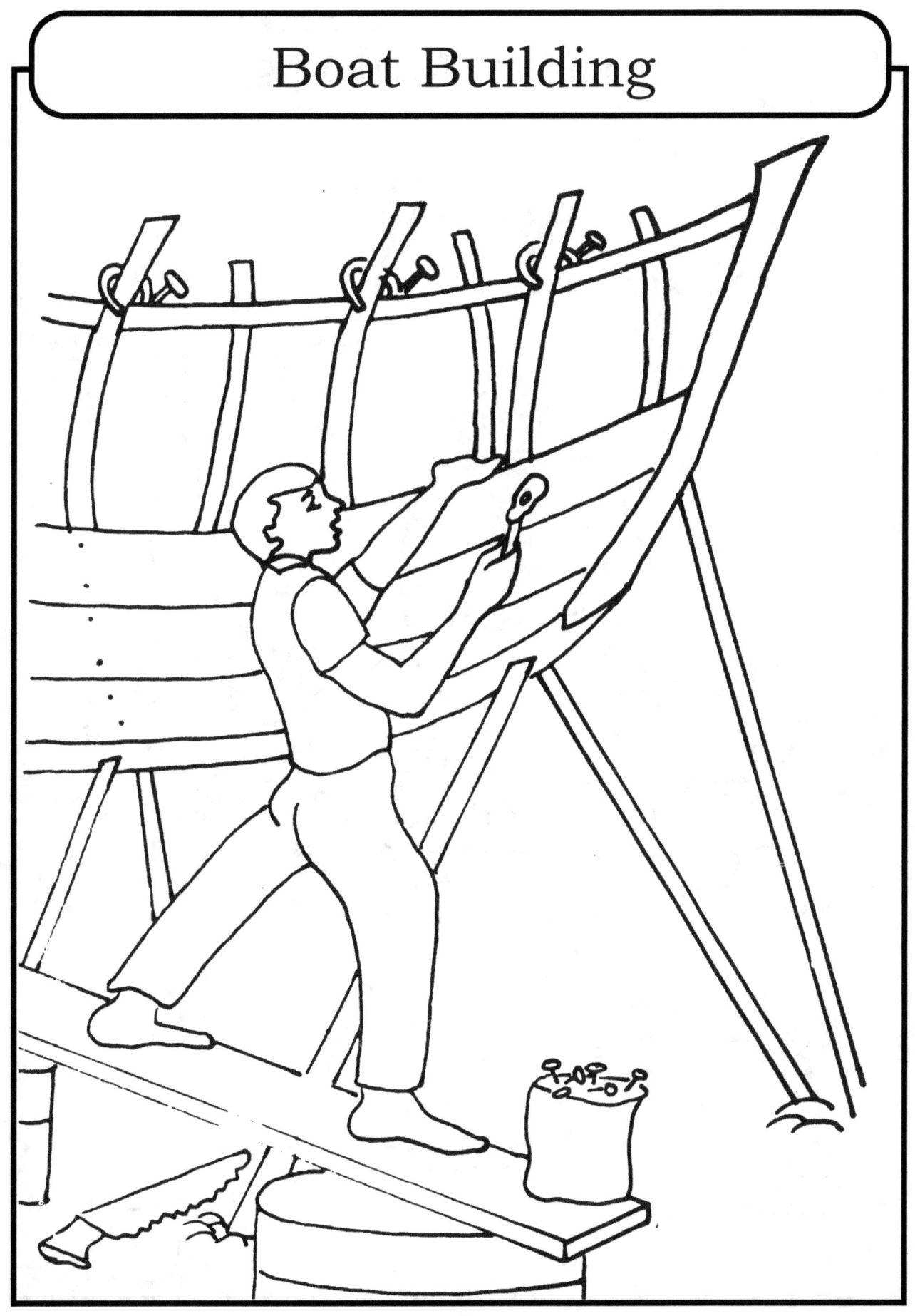

Pottery Making

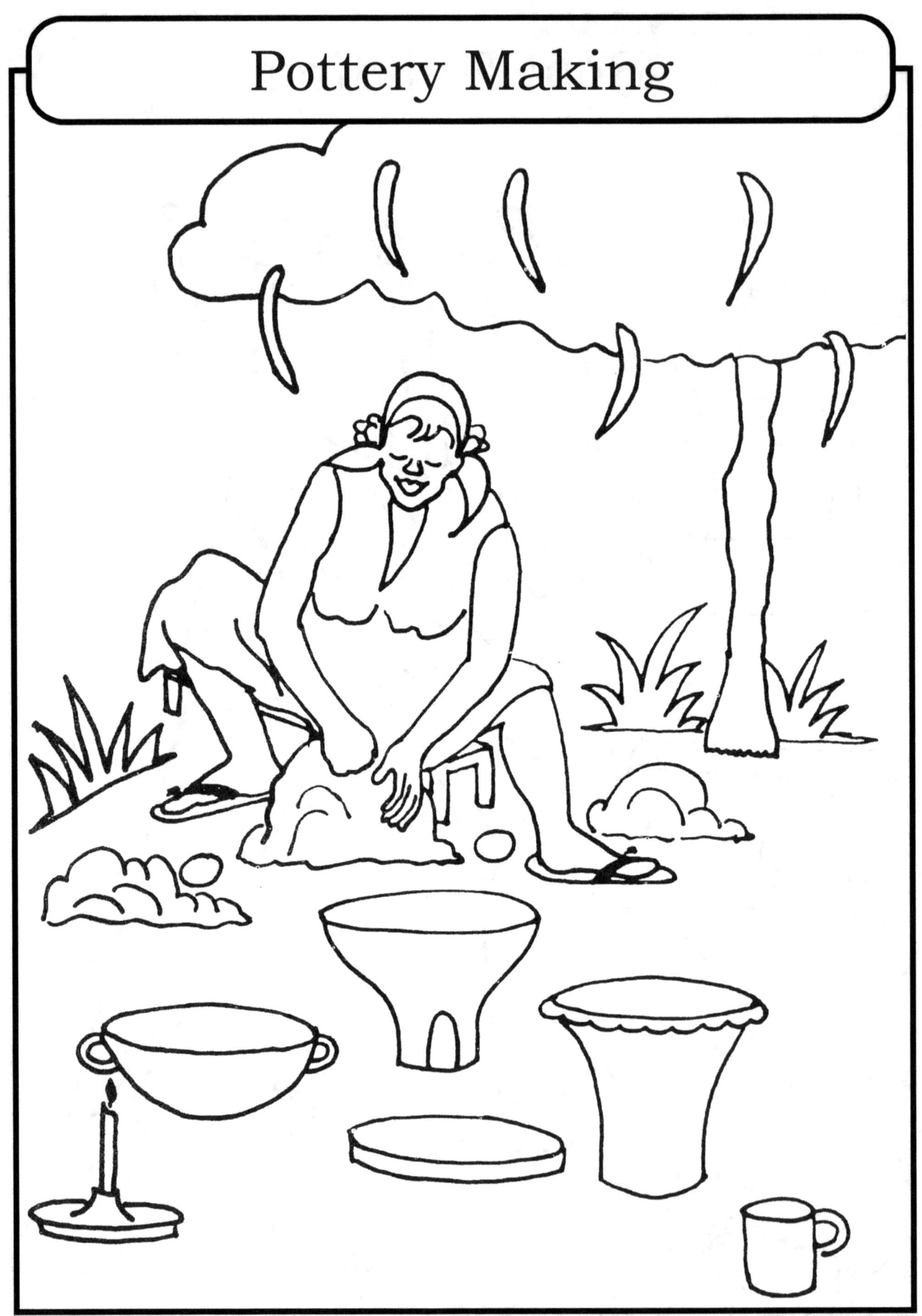

Island String Band

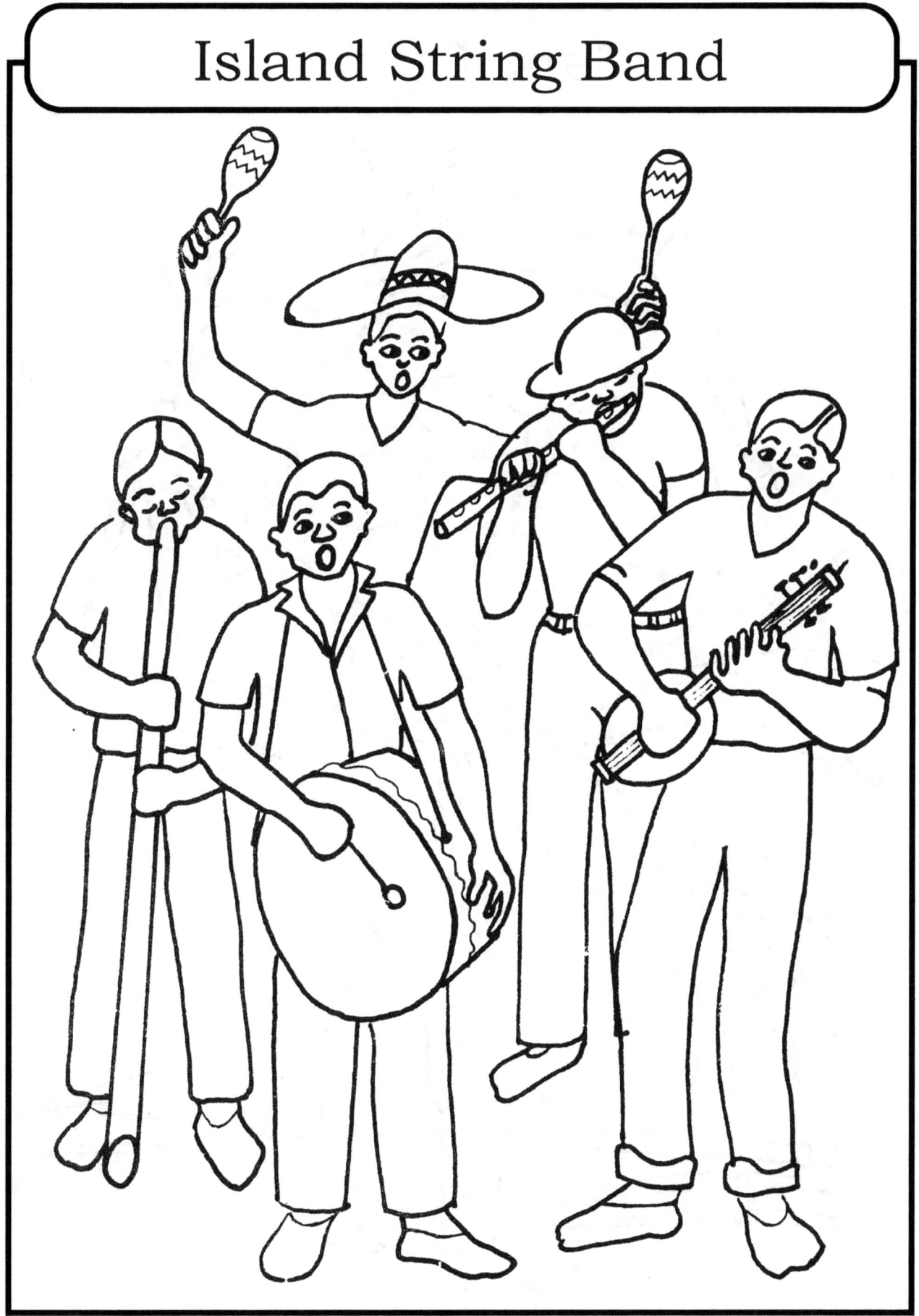

Cane Cutter

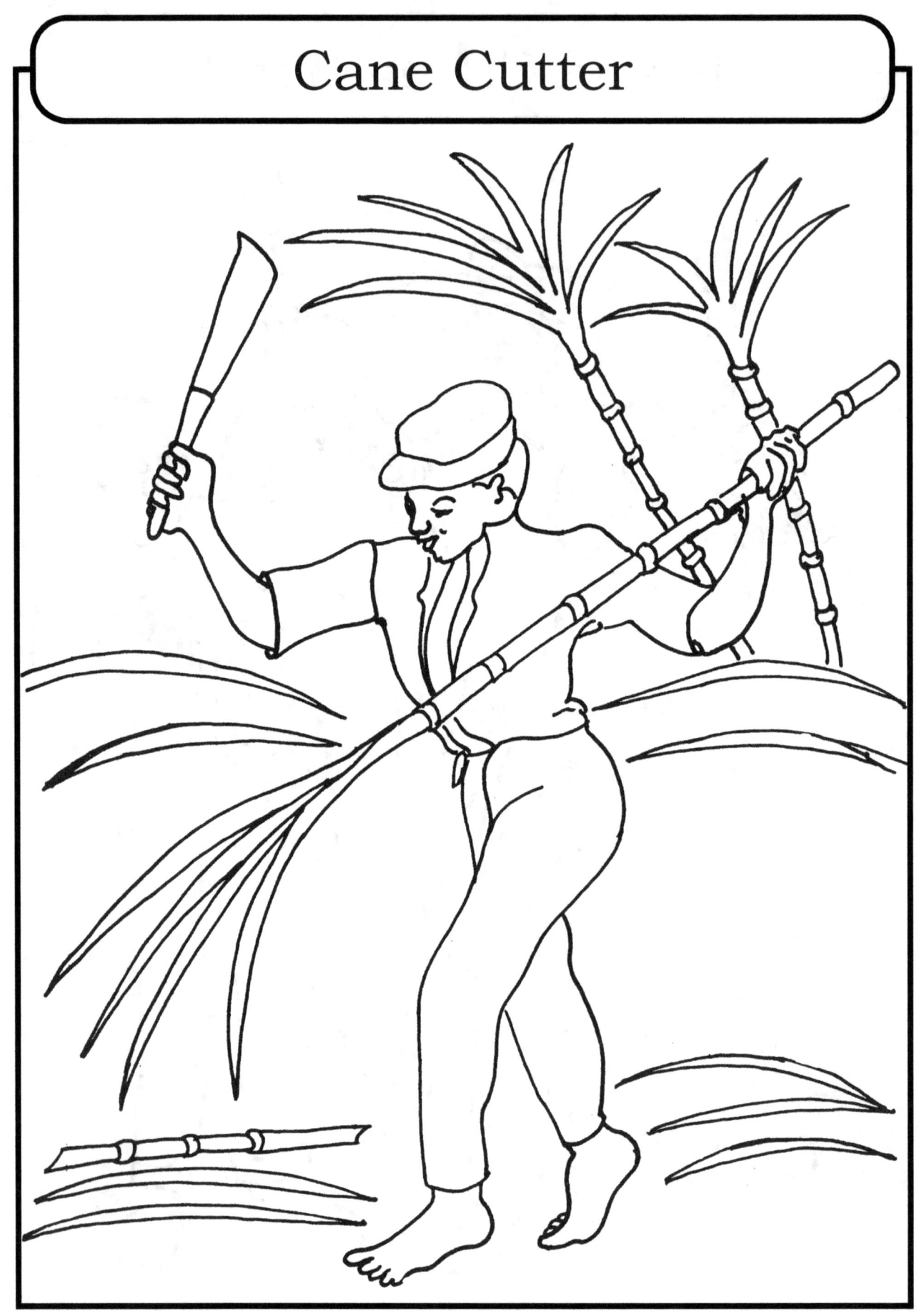

Conch Seller

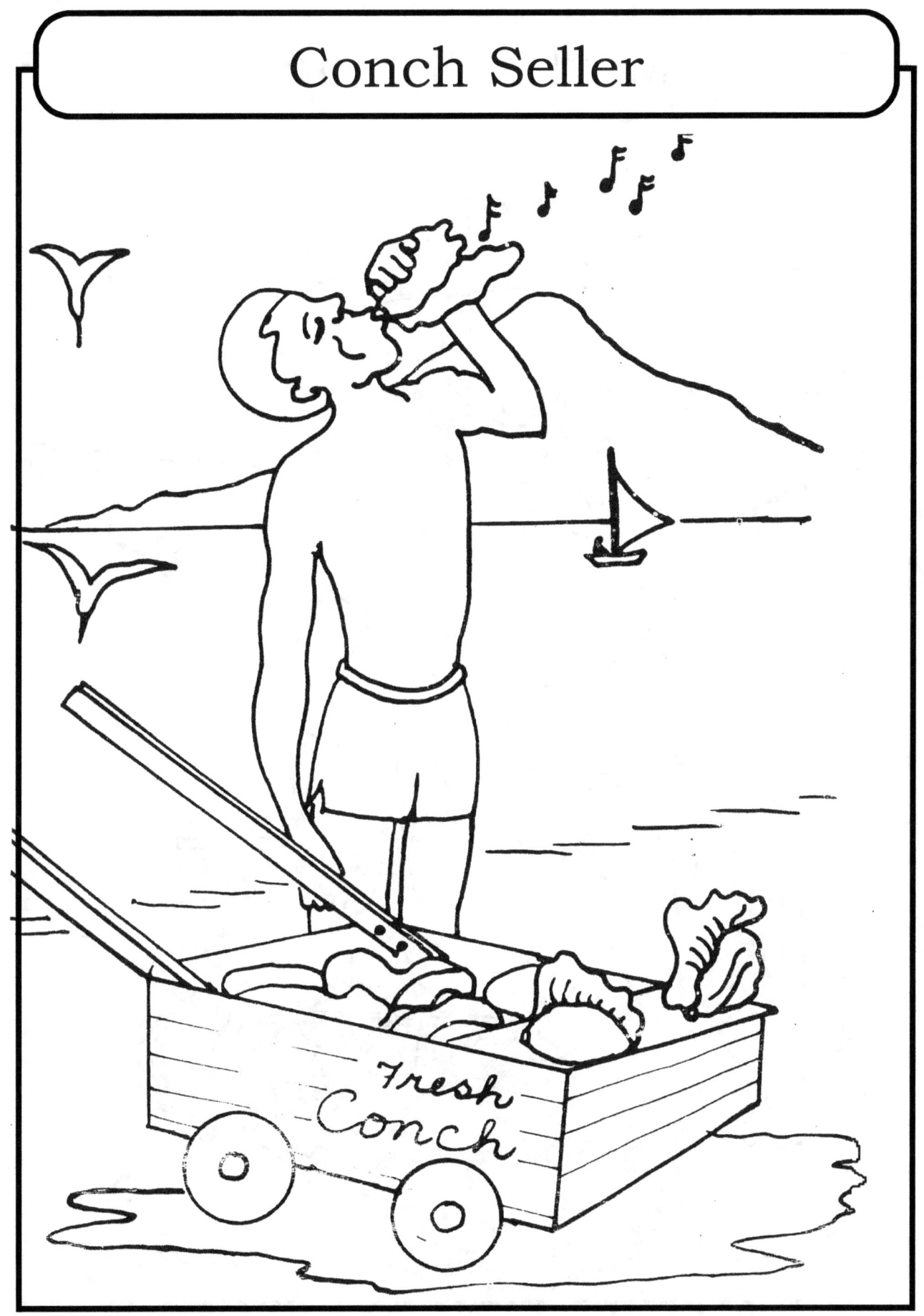

Market Vendor

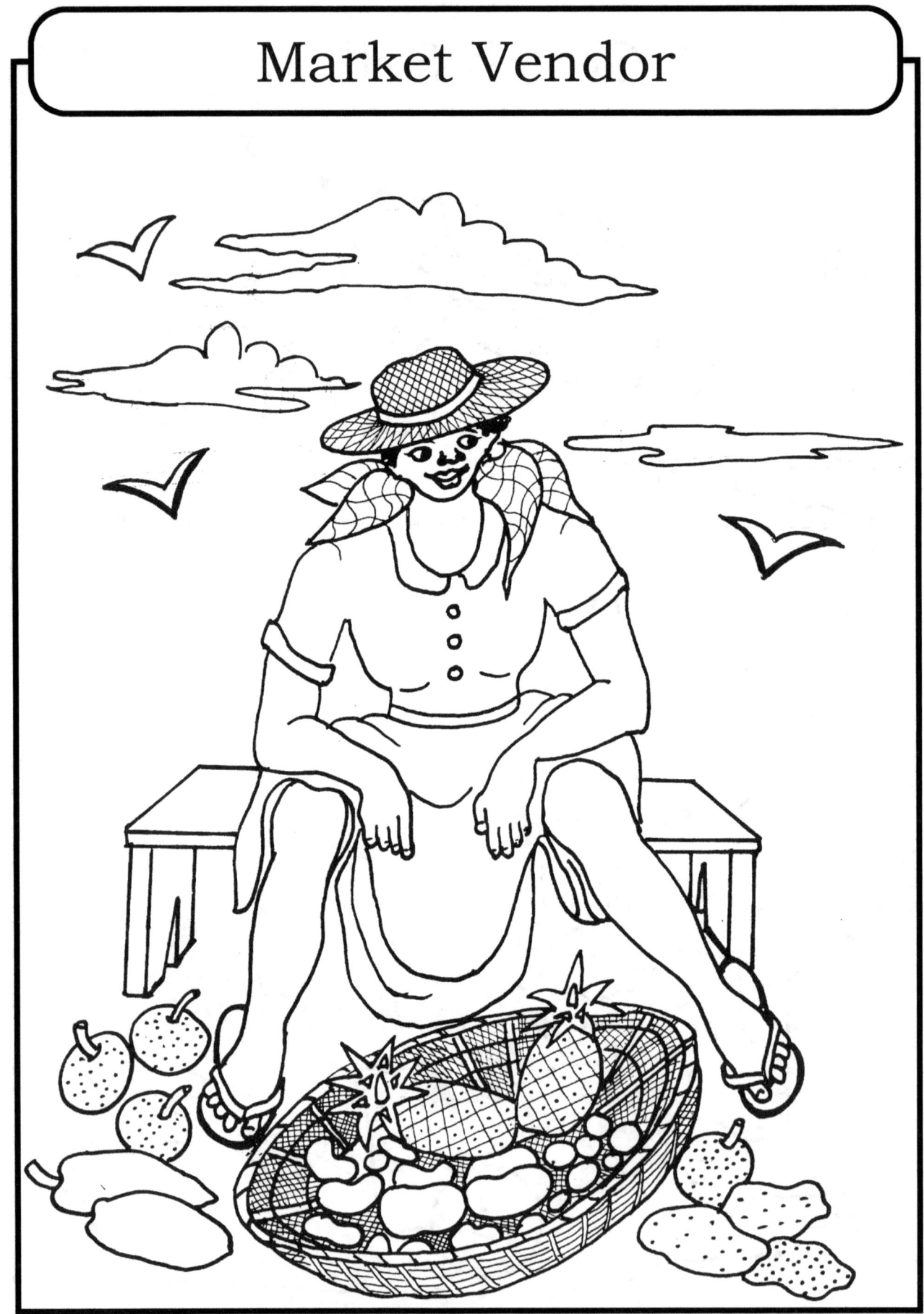

Carnival

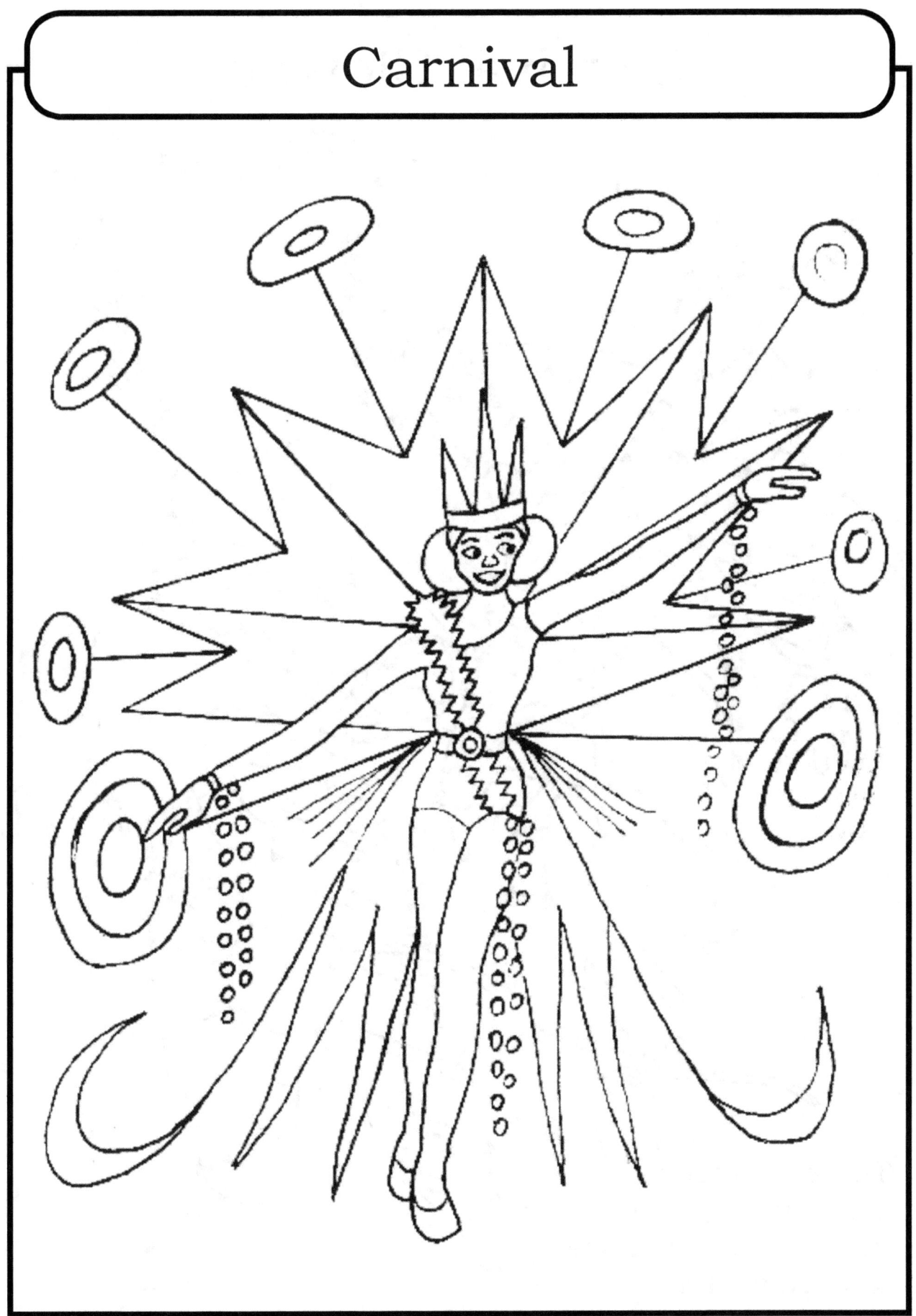

Carnival Clowns

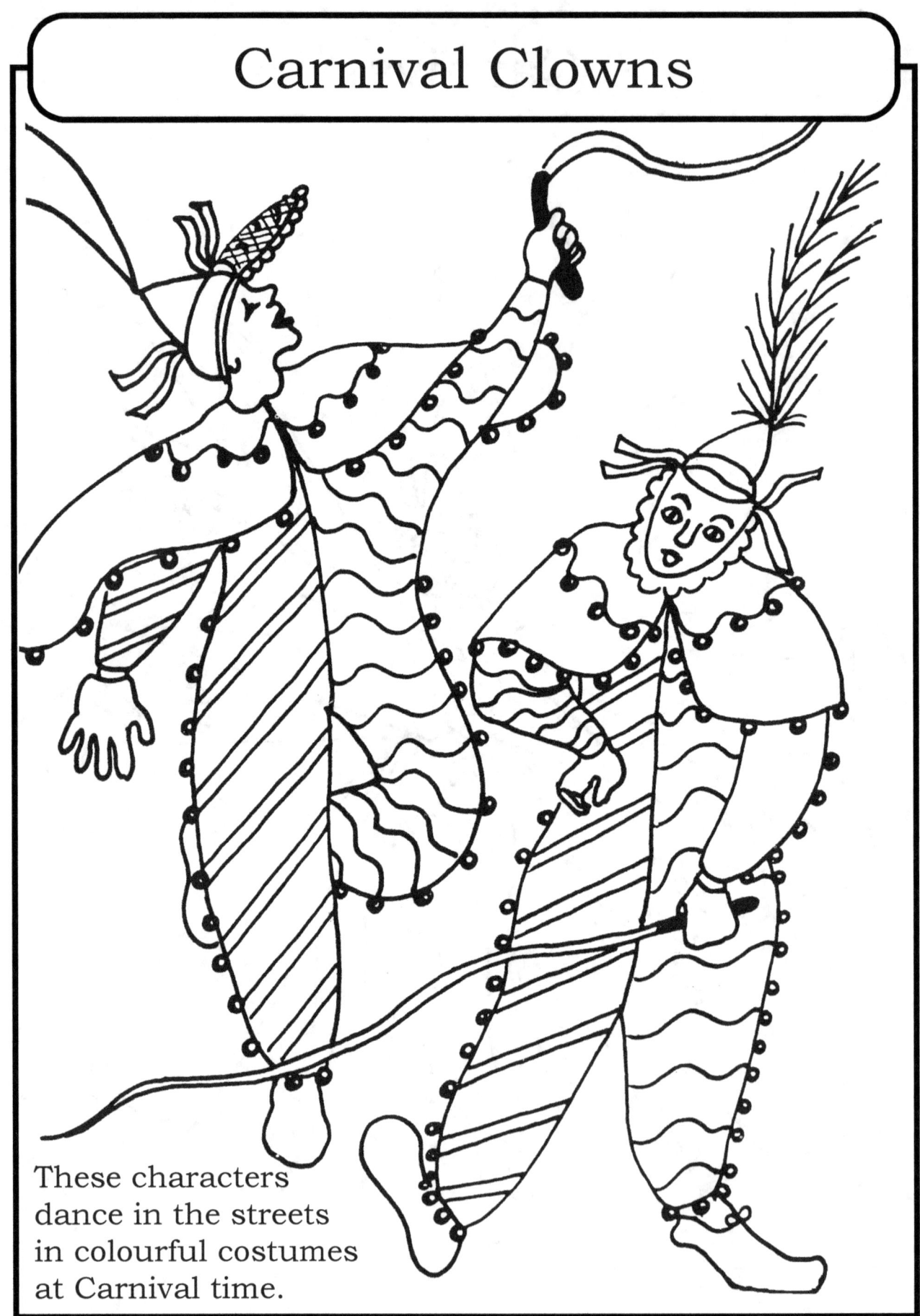

These characters dance in the streets in colourful costumes at Carnival time.

My Memory of St. Kitts-Nevis

Draw Your Own Picture!

www.ingramcontent.com/pod-product-compliance
Lightning Source LLC
Chambersburg PA
CBHW080837170526
45158CB00009B/2576